The
Private Prayers of
POPE
JOHN PAUL II

A Life in Prayer

Joannes Paulus II

The
Private Prayers of
POPE
JOHN PAUL II

A Life in Prayer

ATRIA BOOKS
New York   London   Toronto   Sydney

ATRIA BOOKS
1230 Avenue of the Americas
New York, NY 10020

ISBN: 0-7434-4443-4

First Atria Books hardcover edition 2005

10 9 8 7 6 5 4 3 2 1

ATRIA BOOKS is a trademark of Simon & Schuster, Inc.

Manufactured in the United States of America

For information regarding special discounts for bulk purchases,
please contact Simon & Schuster Special Sales at 1-800-456-6798
or business@simonandschuster.com.

This volume is a selection from the four volumes of *The Private Prayers of Pope John Paul II*, published by Atria Books. The four volumes are: *Words of Inspiration* (2001), *An Invitation to Prayer* (2002), *The Rosary Hour* (2002), and *The Loving Heart* (2003). Each book was originally published in Italian in the Vatican City State. The biographical section is extracted from *Pope John Paul II: The Biography* by Tad Szulc. The epilogue consists of prayers offered by John Paul II after the terrorist attack of September 11, 2001, and parts of his Christmas message of 2002 and an address from March 2003 given to the priests in the Diocese of Rome. As he mentioned in this last speech, the Pope was entering the twenty-fifth year of his pontificate.

CONTENTS

The
Private Prayers of
POPE
JOHN PAUL II

A Life in Prayer

From
John Paul II:
The Biography

By Tad Szulc

1920

Karol Józef Wojtyla was born together with the Polish Miracle. On Tuesday, May 18, 1920, the day of Wojtyla's birth in the small southern Polish town of Wadowice, Marshal Józef Pilsudski was being triumphantly received in Warsaw, the capital of the newly independent Poland, as the conquering hero of the war with the Soviet Union. Only ten days earlier, Pilsudski's young army had seized Kiev, the principal city of the Soviet Ukraine — Poland's first major military victory in over two centuries.

Three months later, on August 15, the Feast of the Assumption of Our Lady, Polish forces commanded by the marshal repulsed at the gates of Warsaw a powerful Soviet counterattack. It became immediately known as the "Miracle on the Vistula," the river bisecting the capital.

The Soviet defeat at Warsaw doomed the advance that, if unchecked, might have continued toward war-shattered Germany and Western Europe, implanting communist rule there. Lenin and Stalin had elaborated a plan to achieve this goal and the Soviets had already occupied Lithuania and Byelorussia in their westward offensive.

The 1920 Miracle on the Vistula was reminiscent of the battle of Vienna in 1683, when the Polish King Jan Sobieski destroyed the Turkish armies of the Grand Vizier, Kara Mustafa, thereby preventing the Ottoman sweep across the face of Europe.

Indeed, Karol Wojtyla and the resurrected Poland, partitioned for 123 years among her three predatory neighbors — Russia, Prussia, and Austria — came to life virtually at the same time.

Karol Jósef Wojtyla

To understand John Paul II, the first non-Italian pope elected in 456 years, one must strive to understand Karol Józef Wojtyla, the man. And to do so, it is crucial to grasp and comprehend the fact of his Polishness. This is the essential trait of his personality, an often disorienting blend of conservatism and modernity.

He is the pontiff of the Universal Church of nearly one billion Roman Catholics and a key player on the world diplomatic scene, but he remains a Polish patriot, a Polish philosopher, a Polish poet, and a Polish politician. During his first papal visit to Poland in June 1979, the embroidered insignia on his chasuble—the orphrey—was the Polish royal crowned white eagle with gold letters on blue proclaiming *Polonia Semper Fidelis* (Poland Always Faithful). At Christmas, he sings Polish carols with Polish friends visiting Rome in an informal family atmosphere. He keeps in touch with the Church and political situation in Poland on a daily basis. In his youth, Wojtyla was an actor in dramas celebrating the cult of Polishness, an experience he fondly remembers to this day.

The pope's philosophical and theological thoughts, his reaction to international occurrences, and his interpretation of history must therefore be examined in the light of his personal background along with his familiarity with world problems and politics, acquired in travel on five continents, his towering intellect and erudition, and his massive literary output.

The son of a deeply patriotic and religious retired career army officer and baptized by a military chaplain, Karol Wojtyla is above all the product of the historical Polish renewal whose foundations are rooted in a sense of national identity. The Roman Catholic Church had helped to preserve it over the centuries through the protection of language and culture—the mystical and messianic spirituality.

But as the prolific poet and playwright that he once was, Woj-

4

tyla may be even better understood in his human dimension than as a philosopher or theologian. His writings reflect his experiences.

Like no other pope, Karol Wojtyla had to work for years as a poverty-stricken manual laborer—under the wartime German occupation of his country. This had the merit of exposing him directly to hardships and experiences in human relationships few other priests had known. It taught him how to suffer in silence and dignity, and instilled in him a habit of absolute discipline, which, as pope, he seeks to impose on an increasingly rebellious Church. Wojtyla has always identified with peasants and workers: it is not uncommon for him to appeal publicly for justice for the "working class," an unusual phrase on the lips of the pope—but one, he says, that dates back to Jesus Christ.

He is also identified with the messianic concept of Polish Catholicism, the national idea and religion being inseparable. As a child (and later as priest and cardinal), Wojtyla was irresistibly attracted to Kalwaria Zebrzydowska, a Bernardine Fathers monastery, thirty miles from his hometown of Wadowice, where tens of thousands of rural inhabitants gathered at Easter to witness the reenactment of the death and resurrection of Christ, and at the Feast of the Assumption of Our Lady in August, the Virgin's taking up into heaven. Kalwaria Zebrzydowska has a Way of the Cross, and crowds of believers moved behind the actor playing Christ from station to station, praying and chanting. It was a monumental display of popular piety, and, as a child, Wojtyla was a part of the Passion Play observance. Later, as a seminarian, he had hoped to become a Discalced Carmelite monk, a most mystical calling, and his first doctoral thesis was on St. John of the Cross, the sixteenth-century Spanish mystic.

On still another level, Wojtyla is the product of great personal tragedy and great personal suffering and loneliness, having lost his entire family before he reached the age of twenty-two: his parents' second-born baby, a girl who died in infancy, his mother when he was eight, his older brother when he was eleven, and his beloved father three months before his twenty-first birthday.

His family tragedies inevitably shaped Wojtyla's character as a man and priest. He speaks of them often in private, especially of his poignant loneliness when his father died. And his proclivity for mysticism and romanticism has given him a sense, if not premonition, of martyrdom. He has been at least four times at the door of death.

The figure Karol Wojtyla always venerated most is Stanisław, the Polish bishop murdered at a church altar in Kraków, then the royal capital, on the orders of a tyrannical king over nine centuries ago. He is now a saint, canonized by the Roman Catholic Church, and a patron saint of Poland. Preparing to leave for Rome to attend the history-making Vatican Council II in 1962, Wojtyla, then a young bishop, told the faithful at Mass in Kraków that "I am leaving the tomb of St. Stanisław for the tomb of St. Peter . . . their greatness is comparable, they complement each other. . . ." He used virtually the same words as cardinal when he left Kraków for the 1978 conclave that would elect him pope.

Today, John Paul II alludes to St. Stanisław when he talks privately about the assassination attempt that almost cost him his life in St. Peter's Square in May 1981. In public comments, he constantly emphasizes that the martyred bishop "always was the patron of moral order in our motherland" and remains "a moral force in our time." Wojtyla, himself Bishop of Kraków for many years, identifies totally with his predecessor, a fervent Polish patriot, at the dawn of the present millennium.

Wojtyla is mystically contemplative, but he is a creature of enormous toughness and stamina, which helped him survive the wounds from the assassin's bullets, major abdominal surgery, serious infections, and numerous accidents over the years, without ever allowing himself to be diverted from the pursuit of his myriad objectives.

Friends who have known Wojtyla over decades insist that prayer and meditation are the principal source of his mental and physical strength and his astonishing capability of restoring his energy — and even his appearance — notwithstanding his punishing schedule at the Vatican and exhausting globe-girdling jet travel. By any normal standards, this is much too much for a man in his mid-eighties, but until recently no one would dare to suggest that he curtail his activities even by a minute a day. John Paul II is a man with a mission, imposing an overwhelming impression that he fears time is running out for him, with so much more still left to accomplish for humanity and his Church. Yet, by mid-1994, his health failing, he had to start cutting back on his schedule. His final drama had begun.

Wojtyla is said to pray as many as seven hours a day: at his private chapel at dawn, sometimes prostrate before the altar, then with invited guests before breakfast, often in his study next to his bedroom, at Masses and services in Rome or on the road, aboard the plane, and on the back seat of his black Mercedes limousine. The pope has a power of concentration that wholly insulates him from his temporal surroundings as he slides into prayer or meditation, even facing huge crowds at an outdoor Mass. The expression on his broad face is otherworldly, he shuts his eyes so tight that he seems to be in pain, and, occasionally, his lips move lightly in silent prayer. Then the moment passes, and Wojtyla is alert again, the happy smile is back on his face, and his eyes scan the clergy and the rows of faithful in front of him.

Addressing university students at a Kraków church in 1972, as cardinal, Wojtyla preached that prayer "is a conversation," but it also means "contact with God," and then went on to explain in his methodical way: "Human prayer has different dimensions, very deep ones. And not only different external dimensions: when, for example, a Moslem prays with his great courage, calling out to his Allah everywhere at prescribed times; when a Buddhist prays, entering complete concentration as if removing himself in that concentration; when a Christian prays, receiving from Christ the word 'Father.'. . . So when I pray, when we pray, then all these roads are as one road, completing one another."

As pope, Wojtyla confided, "When I was young, I thought that prayer could be—should be—only in thankfulness and adoration. A prayer of supplication seemed to me something unworthy. Afterwards I changed my opinion completely. Today I ask very much." When John Paul II comes to pray every morning at his private chapel in the papal apartments, a list of special prayer "intentions," prepared by nuns attached to the household, await him on the prie-dieu. A visitor, hesitatingly inquiring after a private lunch whether the pope would pray for his non-Catholic son-in-law awaiting a heart transplant, was told with great warmth: "Naturally, I shall pray for him. What is his name?"

At the same time, this spiritual pope is an activist and workaholic, busy from before dawn until close to midnight. His bedroom window is the last to turn dark along the façade of the Apostolic Palace that adjoins St. Peter's Basilica. And Wojtyla is a lifetime athlete who gave up skiing, his favorite sport, only after fracturing his hip in a bathroom accident when he was just shy of his seventy-fourth birthday. What turned out to be his farewell skiing trip was an overnight excursion to the Italian mountains north of Rome early in February 1994. The Vatican kept secret the fact that the pope did ski on that occasion because doctors advised against it following a fall in November 1993, when he broke his shoulder. However, he was allowed to hike in the mountains, another of his preferred outdoor activities—but not too much—and he is encouraged by his doctors to swim in the pool at the summer residence at Castel Gandolfo.

His determination to achieve his goals is as steely as his single-mindedness in defending his profoundly conservative theological, ethical, and moral beliefs, so unexpected in an otherwise worldly and modern man. For John Paul II is exceedingly open-minded to new ideas and concepts, from philosophy to science and psychiatry. It was this pope who in 1992 formally pronounced Galileo Galilei innocent of the charges brought against him by the Inquisition three and a half centuries earlier for insisting (heretically, a Church court said in 1633) that the sun *is* the central body of our solar system. As it happened, this notion was first developed by Copernicus, a Polish astronomer known in Kraków as Mikolaj Kopernik. And Wojtyla is captivated by astrophysics and theories on the creation of the universe (he is said to accept the theory of the Big Bang so long as it is recognized that it was God's work). Genetics and its impact on Christian ethics fascinates him, although, in the opinion of scientists at the Vatican, genetics may be as much a controversy for John Paul II's Church as Galileo was for the seventeenth-century papacy.

In preparation for the Third Millennium, John Paul II directed the College of Cardinals to rethink the correctness of the actions of the Church in past centuries, including its stand in religious wars and on the Inquisition, in an undertaking that might, in effect, lead to a fresh version of Roman Catholic history.

The Sistine Chapel (where John Paul II was elected by the College of Cardinals, as most popes have been since the sixteenth century) was restored on his watch, a monumental fourteen-year project. Michelangelo's *Last Judgment,* perhaps the world's greatest artwork, can now be admired in the pure beauty of the colors with which he painted it on the wall of the chapel behind the altar, after completing the famous ceiling frescoes.

John Paul II personally celebrated High Mass at the Sistine Chapel immediately after Easter of 1994, with all the cardinals present in Rome in attendance, to mark the end of the lengthy restoration enterprise.

The Polish pope is a man of touching kindness and deep personal warmth, a quality that evidently he communicates to the hundreds of millions of people who have seen him in person, as he criss-crosses the globe by jet airplane (and hops, skips, and jumps by helicopter from ceremony to ceremony), or on satellite or local television. His smiling face is probably the best known in the world, John Paul II having elevated his mastery of modern communications technology in the service of his gospel to the state of art.

But he really thrives on direct contact with people—individuals or huge crowds—which invigorates him even at moments of utter physical fatigue. In public, he likes to joke, often in a slightly self-deprecatory fashion, in whatever language he happens to be using at the time, and he enjoys the crowd's laughing, applauding responses. It may be the actor in him.

But notwithstanding his extrovert public persona, Wojtyla is a very private man who keeps even those closest to him at arm's length, sometimes imperceptibly. He possesses a very private sense of humor, which he displays at intimate moments, complete with a mischievous glint in his gray-blue eyes and, sometimes, a remark that quite pointedly goes to the heart of the matter—not always in a way complimentary to the person under consideration.

At a lunch or dinner in the plain dining room in the Papal Apartments at the Apostolic Palace—on the third floor—with only a single guest and his two private secretaries, the pope is an amiable host, conducting the conversation in a fashion so relaxed that the visitor quickly forgets that he is in the presence of His Holiness. There are no formalities about second helpings or accepting a second (or third) glass of wine—Wojtyla likes to add a touch of water to his wine—and the meal, an interesting mix of Italian and Polish cuisine prepared by Polish nuns and served by the pope's Italian valet, is abundant; the host himself eats heartily between smiles and makes comments on a variety of themes. It is difficult not to like him.

From earliest childhood, Wojtyla had displayed an extremely rare but wholesome devotion to God and religion that may suggest in retrospect that he is a "chosen one," if, indeed, God works in this way. Family tragedies were an added component in strengthening his faith. Polish traditions of mysticism and messianism, surrounding him as a youth, inevitably played a crucial role in turning him toward the priesthood. In fact, Wojtyla was directly involved with the Church and its organizations and activities from his youngest years, not as convenient pietism in a religion-oriented society, but as a perfectly natural and logical endeavor for him. A succession of dramatic events and astounding coincidences, bordering on the mystical, occurred during the period preceding the start of his secret theological studies.

As priest, Karol Wojtyla threw himself joyfully into the practice of his calling, deeper and deeper theological and philosophical studies and reflection, and an enormous workload. His spiritual and intellectual qualities and his warm and attractive personality were noticed higher up in the Church where he was able to command vital support along with the friendship of his secular and clerical contemporaries.

Wojtyla always had powerful protectors and advocates—from Kraków's Archbishop (and later Cardinal) Adam Stefan Sapieha, even before he entered the underground seminary, to Pope Paul VI, who held him in the highest esteem, powerfully aiding his ecclesiastic career. His rise in the Church was meteoric.

The entire trajectory of Karol Wojtyla's life adds up to a formidable project to improve himself in preparation for a predestined future or, simply, for God's greater glory.

No bishop or cardinal in recorded memory has toiled harder as pastor, scholar, intellectual, and de facto political leader (in and out of the Church) than Wojtyla in the prepontifical period. It took thirty-two years for him to traverse the distance from the Kraków priesthood to the Holy See, achieving it at the fairly young age of fifty-eight, with every year bringing fresh accomplishments. In education and erudition as well as in theological, philosophical, and literary output in the formative period, he could be compared only to Gregory the Great, who became pope at age fifty in A.D. 590. He would resemble Gregory, too, in "inexorable severity."

Wojtyla began composing remarkably good poetry in his late teens, appeared at sixteen in the first amateur theatrical play in Wadowice (a Polish messianic drama that he also co-directed), and wrote two biblical dramas at twenty. He spoke fluent Latin and read Greek and German when he graduated from high school. He was awarded his first doctorate (in mystical theology) at twenty-two and his second (in philosophy, accentuating his beloved phenomenology) at thirty-two. His first "political" newspaper article (on French worker-priests) was published when he was twenty-nine.

He served as a Kraków university chaplain and taught ethics at three Polish theological seminaries and at Lublin Catholic University, making friends and impressing people in all walks of life wherever he went. He made lifetime friends among workers at the Kraków quarry and chemical plant where he was a wartime laborer (and simultaneously a secret seminarian), remembering them fondly by name when he was cardinal. As student, worker, priest, or actor, Wojtyla was always the most popular person in his milieu.

A bishop at thirty-eight, he began to be known in Kraków, in Poland, in Rome, and throughout the Church worldwide. A fine, instinctive politician in the best sense of the word, Wojtyla started to build a potential constituency (consciously or not) through more and more key friendships in the Church. He shone at Vatican Council II, delivering six intellectually puissant speeches in impeccable Latin. An increasingly frequent visitor in Rome with growing involvement in the activities of the Curia, he was soon noticed by Pope Pius VI, being named cardinal at forty-seven.

Speaking a half-dozen foreign languages (Italian, Spanish, German, and French being his best), Wojtyla traveled all over Western Europe and attended international Church meetings in the United States, Canada, and Australia, accepting invitations whenever Polish communist authorities were willing to grant him a passport. Everywhere, he befriended cardinals and bishops. At the same time, he regularly invited foreign cardinals and bishops, many of them from the Third World (which would become very important at the right time) to visit him in Kraków, where they could observe his tireless pastoral labors.

Before long, Wojtyla was the most important figure in the Polish episcopate, after the aging, old-fashioned Cardinal Stefan Wyszyński of Warsaw, the Primate of Poland. There seemed to be no subject that did not captivate his attention: he organized symposia and conferences of theologians, philosophers, scientists, physicians, lawyers, writers, and journalists to learn their subjects and their concerns as they affected Polish society. As pope, he transplanted this system to the Vatican (and the Castel Gandolfo residence during the summer). He knew then and he knows now how to listen.

Was it therefore logical — or predestined — that with this magnificent preparation Karol Wojtyla would crown his life as pope?

1967

In 1967, at the young age of forty-seven, Karol Wojtyla seemed to have reached the top of his ecclesiastic career.

The cardinalate is a lifetime appointment, although cardinals, under rules established by the Second Vatican Council, must retire from governing, pastoral, or administrative activities at seventy-five. But they remain members of the College of Cardinals, being most pleasantly pensioned off, and they can vote in a conclave for a new pontiff until the age of eighty.

For Cardinal Wojtyla, this meant, in practical terms, that he was guaranteed full-time occupation and great Church and political power for the next twenty-eight years. Because he was the governing Metropolitan Archbishop of Kraków, which is a function independent of the cardinalate title and prestige, he was the second most powerful and influential Church leader in Poland after Primate Wyszyński, and many churchmen believed that in fact Wojtyla had more quiet influence.

Wojtyla was, of course, deeply engaged in policymaking in the Polish episcopate and he was increasingly drawn by Pope Paul VI into Holy See matters. He was a Kraków-based Polish celebrity. Still, there were limitations on what he could do and say. His admirable and absolute loyalty to Primate Wyszyński, notwithstanding Wojtyla's deep but silent reservations about the man and his ideas, was the principal limit—self-imposed—on his freedom of action and speech, aside from the observance of normal hierarchical deference.

Did Karol Wojtyla ever think that he might be pontiff of the Roman Catholic Church?

Obviously, he had heard the idea—or hope—mentioned on innumerable occasions, from Father Pio in Italy in 1947, to a little girl in the town of Ludźmierz six weeks after he was anointed cardinal. A friend described the event in a memoir preserved in the archives of the Kraków archdiocese: "A little girl, welcoming the cardinal, recited a poem in which the final words expressed the expectation that he would now become pope. This caused general merriment. The Cardinal did not laugh. He leaned down gravely and kissed the little girl on the forehead."

As a practical matter, papal prospects for him were dim at that stage, except for reasons of age. Though longevity has characterized popes in this century—both Pius XII and John XXIII died in their eighties—Paul VI was already seventy when he named Wojtyla cardinal in 1967. Even if he, too, lived past his eightieth birthday (which he would), Wojtyla would still be extremely young by pontifical standards.

The real problems were that the idea of a non-Italian pope was still very farfetched (although Paul VI had mentioned it once) and that, at least when measured in 1967, Wojtyla had not yet acquired the necessary stature to be a plausible conclave candidate notwithstanding the excellent reputation he had acquired during the Second Vatican Council. He would use well the eleven years of cardinalate that lay ahead to augment this stature.

1978

Monday, October 16, the first order of business (after the morning Mass) was for the non-Italians to persuade the College of Cardinals that the time had come for a foreign pope. And Wojtyla supporters, now in growing numbers, had to make it plain—delicately—that he was the man.

Cardinal König [Cardinal Franz König of Vienna] rose at the morning plenary session to make the basic case before his fellow electors. This is how he remembers the occasion: "I recall that before the previous conclave, I got several letters from unknown people in Italy, saying, 'Please vote for a non-Italian because our country is in such a mess, and it would help us if a non-Italian becomes pope.' A very curious argument. So, at the beginning, in my opinion, the reason [for the opposition to Wojtyla] was that he was young, and, much more than that, a non-Italian coming from an Eastern country."

König was making the point that while the cardinals realized that a younger pope was desirable, Wojtyla, only fifty-eight at that time, seemed too young to many. This view was shared by Primate Wyszyński who, at seventy-seven, embarrassed some of his friends by suggesting during Sunday night Sistine Chapel conversations that *he* would be the "natural" foreign pontiff—if it came to that. Actually, the primate, who always had very mixed feelings about Wojtyla, believed, rather surprisingly, that the next pope should be an Italian. His biographer recounts that Wyszyński "thought that tradition would be respected in the election of another Italian pope. . . . What is more, he regarded such an outcome as fitting: not only did he think the Romans should have an Italian bishop, but he also feared the consequences of violating a 455-year-old tradition."

Such, then, was the resistance König and his allies had to overcome. As he recalls the Monday morning session, "I defended my opinion openly before the conclave. I said that 'it's time to change the system and to vote for a non-Italian. That is my opinion.'"

After two ballots Monday morning, there still was no pope and, once more, black smoke poured out the chimney of the Sistine Chapel to the disappointment of the tens of thousands of the faithful in St. Peter's Square. Having no idea what was happening inside, the crowd was growing increasingly tense and worried. But as they sat down to lunch, the cardinals had finally made up their minds that they would pick a foreigner. Still, the question was, "Who?"

As the Monday afternoon session opened, it was obvious that there were only four plausible foreign candidates: Wojtyla, who had received a few votes even on Sunday afternoon; König, who definitely did not want the job; Cardinal Eduardo Francisco Pironio of Argentina (who was fifty-eight); and Cardinal Johannes Willebrands of the Netherlands, sixty-nine, who had earned much respect for his work in the realms of religious liberty and ecumenical unity among Christian churches. Willebrands, in fact, received twenty votes Monday morning before shifting his own support to Wojtyla.

Cardinal Enrique y Tarancón recalled that "at noon of the second day I realized that it would be Wojtyla." He added that "the first day—Sunday—after four ballots, the cardinals were a bit disoriented, but on Monday morning we felt it would be Karol Wojtyla. We had seen on the first day that it couldn't be an Italian, so we had to search for a new way, and on the second day it was clear where we were going."

Belgian Cardinal Suenens said that "on the second day, there wasn't too much discussion. It became the language of mathematics. And Karol Wojtyla was the most evident name."

But the first ballot Monday afternoon—the seventh of the conclave—did not produce Wojtyla's victory. He was still short of the magic seventy-five votes. More black smoke. Cardinal Krol [Cardinal John Krol of Philadelphia] had brought around the Americans, and Cardinal Joseph Ratzinger, the conservative German theologian, delivered the votes of the Germans, who in the morning had declined to go for the Pole. Brazil's Lorscheider, Argentina's Pironio, and Benin's Bernardin Gantin mobilized Latin American and African votes. But most of the Italians were still denying Wojtyla their twenty-five votes, and the outcome remained in doubt as the cardinals got ready for the afternoon's second vote.

The problem was to make Wojtyla fully acceptable to all the Church factions and, evidently, this required a formidable last-moment effort. As Cardinal Enrique y Tarancón put it, "We were not looking for a conservative or a progressive, but someone 'sure' in line with Vatican Council II. It was not in ideological terms. Besides, Wojtyla was a pastoral bishop, which was vital."

Cardinal Eugène Tisserant, the white-bearded Dean of the College of Cardinals, called for the eighth ballot shortly after 5:00 P.M. The tension inside the Sistine Chapel was unbearable; many feared an unbreakable deadlock over the Italian question, which would plunge the Church into a profound crisis. König said that "there was enormous tension the whole time."

Then the break came. Cardinal Sebastiano Baggio, the powerful Italian Prefect of the Congregation for Bishops, decided to back Wojtyla, followed by just enough recalcitrant Italian cardinals. As votes were called out by the counters, the cardinals wrote down the numbers on their pads. König, who sat directly ahead of Wojtyla, recalls that "when the number of votes for him approached one-half [of the needed total], he cast away his pencil and sat up straight. He was red in the face. Then he was holding his head in his hands."

König went on to say: "My impression was that he was completely confused. Then the final majority number turned up. He had two-thirds of the votes plus one. . . ."

As the ballot reached ninety-four for him—seventeen cardinals refused to accept him—Wojtyla leaned down over the desk and began writing furiously.

At 6:18 P.M., Cardinal Tisserant announced in the chapel that Karol Wojtyla of Kraków had been elected pontiff of the Roman Catholic Church. Cardinal Villot, the chamberlain, approached Wojtyla to ask in Latin: "In accordance with the canon law do you accept?"

Wojtyla had no hesitation. "It is God's will," he replied. "I accept."

The cardinals broke out in applause. Cardinal Enrique y Tarancón summed up later what had just happened in the Sistine Chapel: "God forced us to break with history to elect Karol Wojtyla."

In the back of the chapel, Cesare Tassi's stove spewed out white smoke to the world. It announced that a pope had been chosen, but his identity was not made known at that moment. Suspense gripped St. Peter's Square as night fell.

Taking the name of John Paul II—out of respect for his predecessor—Karol Wojtyla became the 263rd successor of St. Peter, the 264th pope of his Church, and thereby head of seven hundred million Roman Catholics, the single largest and oldest religious institution in the world.

As pope, he also became "The Bishop of Rome, the Vicar of Jesus Christ, the Successor of St. Peter, Prince of the Apostles, the Supreme Pontiff who has the primacy of jurisdiction and not merely of honor over the Universal Church, the Patriarch of the West, the Primate of Italy, the Archbishop and Metropolitan of the Roman Province, the Sovereign of the State of Vatican City, Servant of the Servants of God." He was to be addressed as "His Holiness the Pope" or, more informally, as "Holy Father."

At the age of fifty-eight and a half years (almost to the day), the rugged, athletic Polish cardinal, standing five feet ten and a half inches, was the youngest pope since 1846, and, of course, the first foreigner since 1523. And John Paul II wasted no time demonstrating to the cardinals and then to the rest of the world that he would be a very different kind of pope.

As soon as Karol Wojtyla accepted the papacy, Cesare Tassi, the Sistine official, led him out of the chapel through a small door to the left of the altar, below *The Last Judgment,* to a whitewash-walled narrow room to don the white papal vestments awaiting the new pontiff (actually, the room held three sets of vestments in portmanteaus: in small, medium, and large sizes, to fit whoever was chosen).

Returning to the chapel, Wojtyla found an armchair placed in front of the altar where, according to tradition, he would sit to receive the cardinals' vows of obedience. But, as Cardinal Enrique y Tarancón recalled, Wojtyla had other ideas.

"When the Master of Ceremonies invited the pope to sit down," he said, "Wojtyla replied, 'No, I receive my brothers standing up. . . .' " One by one, the cardinals came to Wojtyla to be embraced by him. The longest embrace was for Primate Wyszyński. Then the cardinals sang the *Te Deum.* The ceremony in the chapel lasted nearly one hour (the paper ballots were burned at the same time to assure eternal secrecy over the election proceedings).

Next, Wojtyla left the Sistine Chapel through the back door, past the partition, leading the papal procession across the vast Regal and Ducal Halls of St. Peter's Basilica to the Loggia, the central balcony overlooking the vast darkened square filled with over two hundred thousand faithful — Italians, foreign pilgrims, and tourists.

Cardinal Felici was the first to step out on the balcony at 6:44 P.M. as the great cross on the façade of the basilica lit up and the Swiss Guards marched into the square, the band playing and the huge papal flag unfurled. In sonorous Latin, Felici shouted: "I announce to you a great joy. . . . We have a Pope!—*Habemus Papam!*"

As the first roar of the crowd died down, Felici identified him: "Carolum Sanctae Romanae Ecclesiae Cardinalem Wojtyla . . . Ionnaem Paulum Secundum!"

Silence swept St. Peter's Square. Wojtyla was a totally unknown name to the multilingual crowd. People looked at one another questioningly, wondering who was this Wojtyla? An African? No, someone said, "He's Polish!"

Now John Paul II, red chasuble over his white robe, the papal cross over his chest, and a happy smile over his broad face, moved forward to bestow his first "Urbi et Orbi" (City and World) blessing. It was 7:20 P.M. But first, departing from custom, he delivered a brief address in Italian:

> May Jesus Christ be praised! . . . Dearest brothers and sisters, we are still grieved after the death of our most beloved Pope John Paul I. And now the most eminent cardinals have called a new bishop of Rome. They have called him from a distant country, distant but always so close through the communion in the Christian faith and tradition. . . .
>
> I do not know whether I can explain myself well in your — our Italian language. If I make a mistake you will correct me. And so I present myself to you all to confess our common faith, our hope, our confidence in the Mother of Christ and of the Church, and also to start anew on this road of history and of the Church, with the help of God and with the help of men.

It was, in effect, his acceptance speech — his bid to be accepted as a non-Italian pope in Italy — and he had drafted it in the Sistine Chapel after the cardinals' votes for him had exceeded seventy-five. And John Paul II found that he was accepted in Italy and across a fascinated world with extraordinary speed and ease. He also imposed himself instantly upon the Church and the Roman Curia.

As he faced the great Roman crowd in St. Peter's Square, Monsignor Dziwisz, his chaplain and secretary, scurried across the city to bring the pope's meager belongings from his Polish College apartment on Piazza Remuria to the temporary lodgings in the Apostolic Palace where he would spend the first night as pontiff.

* * *

John Paul II concentrated on what were for him four immensely important activities on Tuesday, October 17, his first full day as pope.

In the morning, he concelebrated solemn Mass at the Sistine Chapel with all the cardinals, again bestowing the "Urbi et Orbi" blessing.

In the afternoon, he was driven in the black Mercedes papal limousine to the Gemelli Polyclinic to visit his paralyzed friend, Bishop Deskur. "He taught me how to be pope," John Paul II said as he walked into Deskur's room. A crowd had gathered in the clinic's corrdiors for a glimpse of him, but the pope had to be reminded that they expected a blessing. Smiling sheepishly, he made the sign of cross, remarking, "I'm not used to it yet. . . ."

In the late afternoon, John Paul II received Polish friends at an informal ceremony he called "Farewell to the Motherland" in a room behind the stage of the Paul VI Auditorium next to the basilica. Each friend was summoned individually over a loud-speaker to come to greet the pope. Jerzy Kluger, Wojtyla's Jewish friend and classmate from Wadowice high school, and his English wife were the first to be called.

In the evening, Wojtyla gave orders for his cardinal's red zuc-chetto — skullcap — to be placed at the altar of the Polish Virgin of Ostrabrama in Vilnius in Soviet Lithuania. It had to be smuggled there.

That was how the pontificate of John Paul II began.

Pope John Paul II

1979

John Paul II landed in Warsaw on the morning of June 2, 1979, eight months to the day after he had left as Cardinal Wojtyla for the Vatican conclave, and from the moment he knelt to kiss the

21

Polish ground at Okecie Airport, he lived nine days of national ecstasy.

At least ten million Poles (of a population of thirty-five million) saw him in person in the nine cities, towns, and sanctuaries where he appeared, prayed, and spoke before the masses of humanity. The country had exploded in color: white-and-red Polish flags and white-and-yellow papal flags were everywhere, and portraits of a smiling Wojtyla decorated with papal pennants seemed to be in every window along the routes of his motorcades. His appearances drew the biggest crowds in Polish history.

Others watched him on Polish state television although the ever-zealous party officials had ordered their cameramen to keep the lenses on John Paul II in tight shots and avoid showing the huge throngs in attendance at Mass and other events. It was foolish totalitarian behavior because every citizen knew that millions had turned out to cheer the pontiff and intone the ancient song, "We want God!" Poles spoke of "our nine days of freedom."

The pope set the tone for his visit—his second foreign papal trip—with admirable diplomatic deftness, again blending the spiritual and the temporal in defining his Polish mission as well as his overall policies. Responding to airport welcoming remarks by President Henryk Jablon̈ski, John Paul II announced that "my visit is dictated by strictly religious motivation" although "I earnestly hope that [it] will serve the great cause of closeness and cooperation among nations . . . mutual understanding, reconciliation and peace in the contemporary world . . . [and] the internal unity of my compatriots. . . ."

Religion and patriotism always went hand in hand in Polish history, and the pope elevated the sentiment to magnificent heights on Jasna Góra—the Luminous Mountain—at Częstochowa, the shrine of the Black Madonna, the Queen of Poland. He went there after appearances in Warsaw and Gniezno, the see of the oldest Polish diocese. Spending three days in the Częstochowa-Jasna

Góra area, John Paul II spoke *twenty-three* times—surely a record in papal annals—before audiences ranging from sealike crowds at solemn Mass to groups of fathers and mothers superior of male and female religious orders, the Polish Episcopal Conference, young people, and the sick and the infirm.

And the pope's homilies and speeches from the most hallowed ground in Poland were not the usual sort, pious exhortations to which worshippers there were accustomed. Some were lengthy and complex essays on Polish history in the context of Częstochowa's salvation by the Madonna from besieging Swedish armies in the seventeenth century—but moving into the modern age as well—or in the context of St. Stanisław, his martyrdom, and human freedom. Others were lectures on the state of the Church following the Second Vatican Council. As an American reporter wrote from Częstochowa: "Every papal gesture, every deft historical reference had political connotations in this setting."

Thus John Paul II had come back to Poland as preacher and teacher, historian and patriot, philosopher and theologian. It was his greatest tour de force to date, and he was only halfway through the Polish pilgrimage.

But the most personal and emotionally charged part of Wojtyla's Polish homecoming was the return to his archdiocese: Kraków, Kalwaria Zebrzydowska, Wadowice, Oświecim, Nowy Targ. . . .

And adoring throngs turned out to welcome him home, filling every square foot of the sprawling, triangular Blonia Meadow, just east of Jagiellonian University and the Old Town, where he spoke lovingly to his fellow Krakowians, calling the city "this Polish Rome." He talked nostalgically about his Kraków youth, the university, the Nazi occupation, his work at the stone quarry and the Solvay plant, his priestly calling, and his years as bishop and cardinal. His every word was heard in reverent silence, then shouts and applause would soar to the blue spring sky like cannon salvos.

The next day, June 7, John Paul II followed his sentimental

memory route to his favorite Kalwaria Zebrzydowska sanctuary and its Stations of the Cross, reminiscing about his childhood and adult visits there, always drawing inspiration from them. He also recalled that his grandfather and his great-grandfather had served as guides to pilgrims at the sanctuary.

Two hours later, the pope was *really* home — in Wadowice. His old religion teacher and parish priest Edward Zacher greeted him tearfully, and Karol Wojtyla loved every moment in his town, recognizing every person in sight, embracing quite a few, shaking many hands. He praised the local band that played for him, but remarked that "before the war, we oldsters remember but the young know nothing about, we had the superb band of the Twelfth Infantry Regiment. . . ."

After the jokes and laughter of Wadowice came the sorrow and sadness of the Oświecim-Brzezinka concentration camp later that afternoon. Wojtyla had gone there many times in the past, but, as he said during the Mass he celebrated at the camp, "This is a very special sanctuary, and I couldn't have failed to come here as pope." And, once more, John Paul II mentioned St. Stanisław, the nation's first martyr.

Walking slowly along the paths of the camp, preserved intact by the Poles as an eternal memory of the Holocaust, the pope knelt before a stone tablet inscribed in Hebrew, a tablet inscribed in Russian, and a tablet inscribed in Polish. The Hebrew words, he said, "bring to mind the memory of a nation whose sons and daughters were condemned to total extermination. This nation has its beginning with Abraham, who is 'the father of our faith.'. . . And this nation, which received from God Jahwe the Commandment, 'Thou Shall Not Kill,' has itself experienced killing in a particular manner. . . . Nobody may walk past this tablet in indifference. . . ."

A Mass at the market town of Nowy Targ in the foothills of the Carpathians and three more breathless days in Kraków completed John Paul II's Polish pilgrimage. At churches, the Jagiellonian University, and meetings with bishops, theologians, monks, nuns, the young, and the sick, the pope kept up the drumbeat of his message of religious faith and patriotism—and of his devotion to St. Stanisław. In the end, he had had his way, spiritually and politically, in this virtuoso management of his journey.

1981

The horror was the pistol shot fired at John Paul II from less than twenty feet in St. Peter's Square on the afternoon of Wednesday, May 13, 1981, in an assassination attempt by a Turkish terrorist.

The bullet from the powerful 9mm Browning Parabellum penetrated his abdomen, shattering the colon and the small intestine, and went through the sacral vein system. Miraculously, in the words of attending surgeons, the projectile passed a few millimeters from the central aorta. Had it hit the aorta, John Paul II would have died instantly. The bullet missed other vital organs, such as the iliac artery and the ureter, and even nerve centers near them went untouched.

Still, it was touch-and-go during the five hours and twenty minutes of surgery at the Agostino Gemelli Polyclinic, twelve minutes by screaming ambulance from the Vatican. The pope was rushed there from St. Peter's Square within minutes of being struck by one of the two bullets fired by Mehmet Ali Agca in the midst of twenty thousand pilgrims and tourists at the weekly General Audience (the second bullet missed the pontiff altogether). John Paul II had been standing in his open jeep, and Agca had to fire at an upward angle from the pavement.

John Paul II lost consciousness as he reached the hospital, and Monsignor Dziwisz, his private secretary, who was with him during the attack, decided to administer the sacraments of Extreme Unction before the surgery began. When Dr. Francesco Crucitti, the chief surgeon, opened the abdomen, he found it filled with blood, some six pints of it. The sacral system was pouring out blood, the pope's pressure was down to 70 and falling, the pulse had nearly vanished, and Dr. Crucitti realized that his patient had already lost three quarters of his blood.

Stanching the hemorrhage and starting a massive transfusion, he discovered deep lacerations in the colon; it had to be sewn up and twenty-two inches of intestine had to be cut away. Finally, the doctors had to treat the injury to the pope's right shoulder and a finger of his left hand caused by the bullet as it exited his body (two American women tourists standing nearby were badly wounded by the same bullet). And a tooth had been broken during anesthesia.

Monsignor Dziwisz remembered that John Paul II, in great pain after being shot, whispered a short prayer in Polish, "Mary, my mother . . . !" before losing consciousness. He said that the pope later told him that while still conscious, he was certain that his wounds were not fatal and that he would survive. And just a month after the shooting, John Paul II received at his Vatican apartments a Rural Solidarity delegation from Poland, encouraging the farmers in their free trade union struggle and blessing their loaves of bread. His robust constitution and his excellent physical condition helped to speed his recovery.

At his first public appearance in St. Peter's Square after four months of convalescence, John Paul II explained to the crowd of pilgrims that the assassination attempt had been a "divine test" for which he was grateful to God. In his own mystical way, the pope said that "during the last months God permitted me to experience suffering, and the danger of losing my life. He also allowed me to understand clearly . . . that this was one of his special graces for me as a man and at the same time . . . for the Church."

His suffering included a return to the hospital late in June for the treatment of a dangerous cytomegalovirus infection—most likely transmitted with blood during the emergency transfusion— and a second surgical intervention. It was necessary to reverse the colostomy performed as part of the original surgery so that the pope could resume his natural gastric functions. The doctors had wanted to delay the second operation well into August, fearing a cytomegalovirus relapse if done prematurely, but John Paul II insisted on August 5, the Feast of Our Lady of the Snows, in order to be back at the Vatican on August 15, the very important Feast of the Assumption.

The pope had his way, the stitches were taken out on August 13, and he went home the next day. After Assumption, he flew by helicopter to the Castel Gandolfo summer residence to convalesce.

A man who wrote 462 speeches in his first 257 days of papacy (then he slowed down a bit), John Paul II could not stand idleness, even in the hospital with his insides ruptured, and he wasted no time. He met daily with Secretary of State Casaroli to discuss and decide a multitude of matters, worked on the galleys of the *Laborem exercens* encyclical (which would be published on September 14), celebrated Mass in his room, and taped messages to the faithful to be played in St. Peter's Square, starting with the first one on May 18, the fifth day after the shooting and his sixty-first birthday.

In it, John Paul II said: "I am praying for the brother who wounded me and whom I sincerely forgive."

1990

John Paul II has grown increasingly emotional and confrontational in his vision of the world and its ills as he progresses through the eighth decade of his life. He turned seventy on May 18, 1990.

His old Kraków friends say that he had never before displayed such emotionalism, but they believe, as do many observers in Rome and elsewhere, that his attitudes and rhetoric reflect accurately the concerns of many others in the world over the condition of contemporary society.

In this sense, the pope's instincts may be very much attuned to global trends and fears, especially among young people, and his message may fit well into the context of the time toward the end of the century and millennium even if his tone often tends to be messianic, apocalyptic, and verging on hyperbole.

On the mercilessly hot morning of August 15, 1993, the Feast of Assumption, John Paul II summed up his own distress over the present state of the world as he addressed a half million young people gathered at Cherry Creek State Park near Denver for World Youth Day:

A "culture of death" seeks to impose itself on our desire to live and live to the full. There are those who reject the light of life, preferring the "fruitless works of darkness." Their harvest is injustice, discrimination, exploitation, deceit, violence. In every age, a measure of their apparent success is the death of innocents. In our own century, as at no other time in history, the "culture of death" has assumed a social and institutional form of legality to justify the most horrible crimes against humanity: genocide, "final solutions," "ethnic cleansings," and the massive taking of lives of human beings even before they are born or before they reach the natural point of death. . . . Vast sectors of society are confused about what is right and what is wrong, and are at the mercy of those with the power to "create" opinion and impose it on others.

The evening before, during the prayer vigil at the park, the pope expressed grave warnings to his audience:

Christ, the Good Shepherd . . . sees so many young people throwing away their lives in a flight into irresponsibility and falsehood. Drug and alcohol abuse, pornography and sexual disorder, violence: these are grave social problems which call for a social response from the whole of society, within each country and on the international level. . . . In a technological culture in which people are used to dominating matter, discovering its laws and mechanisms in order to transform it according to their wishes, the danger arises of also wanting to manipulate conscience and its demands. In a culture which holds that no universally valid truth is possible, nothing is absolute. Therefore, in the end—they say—objective goodness and evil no longer really matter. Good comes to mean what is pleasing or useful at a particular moment. Evil means what contradicts our subjective wishes. Each person can build a private system of values.

World Youth Days, established by John Paul II in 1986 as formal biennial gatherings to enhance the Church's efforts in pastoral work among young people, have been held, prior to Denver, in Rome, Buenos Aires, Santiago de Compostela in Spain, and Czestochowa, each time in his presence. But the pope has succeeded in making them into joyful occasions rather than simply venues for collective prayer and ominous warnings. At the Colorado state park, for example, there were soloists and combos and a symphony orchestra on the huge stage where John Paul II sat for long hours in an armchair, smiling, waving, and tapping his foot to the music, and occasionally joking into the microphone. Giant closed-circuit television screens above the stage magnified his figure manyfold for those in the vast crowd too far away to see him in person. The mood had seized the audience, there was rhythmic applause, there was the wave.

Colorado being fairly bilingual, a group began chanting, "Juan-Pablo-Segundo: Te-Ama-Todo-El-Mundo!" (John Paul the Second: The Whole World Loves You), which rhymes in Spanish, but the pope interrupted with a mock severe admonition, also in Spanish: "No, no, aquí se habla inglés!" (No, no, English is spoken here!), to the delight of the young crowd.

Conclusion

Theologians, philosophers, and historians — and just plain people around the world who have been touched by John Paul II in some fashion — will debate for years, if not decades, his merits and failures as pontiff of the Roman Catholic Church.

Some will argue that the Polish pope was a great world leader, morally and politically, but that he failed as the head of the Roman Catholic Church. Others will offer differing interpretations as perspective on his papacy increases and more insights are gathered into his work and thought.

In the end, events will define his role as the supreme pastor of his Church and provide judgments of his guidance of Catholicism into the third millennium of the Christian era. There is no question, however, that this man of broad smiles, brooding silences, steely stamina, and endless tenderness for the young, the sick, and humanity will have left a profound impact on our world. There has been no one quite like him in our time.

To know John Paul II, even slightly, is sufficient to sense that he is at peace with himself, his God, and his world in a very simple human fashion.

When he left Kraków for Rome in 1978, with a premonition of the future, Karol Wojtyla observed quietly that a straight line leads from the tomb of St. Stanisław, the martyred Polish bishop, at Wawel Cathedral to the tomb of St. Peter in the basilica in the Vatican. The same straight line leads back from Peter to Stanisław. Wojtyla has never forgotten it.

He always looked homeward.

From
Words of Inspiration

The various vocations in the lay state

The rich variety of the Church is manifested further within each state of life. Thus *within the lay state diverse "vocations" are presented*, or, rather, diverse paths in spiritual life and the apostolate are taken by individual members of the lay faithful. In the area of a "common" lay vocation "special" lay vocations flourish. In this context we should also note the spiritual experience that has developed recently in the Church with the flowering of various forms of Secular Institutes. These offer for the lay faithful, and for priests as well, the possibility of professing the evangelical counsels of poverty, chastity, and obedience through vows or promises, while completely maintaining their own state, lay or clerical. As the synodal Fathers have noted, *"The Holy Spirit generates other forms of self-giving, to which people who remain fully in the lay state can devote themselves."*

We can conclude by rereading a beautiful passage from St. Francis of Sales,* who promoted lay spirituality so well. Speaking of "devotion," or, rather, of Christian perfection, or "life according to the Spirit," he explains in a simple yet insightful way the vocation of all Christians to holiness and, at the same time, the specific form in which individual Christians fulfill it: *"In the creation God commanded the plants to bring forth their fruits, each one 'after its kind.' So does he command all Christians, who are the living plants of his Church, to bring forth the fruits of devotion, each according to his state and his*

---

* Saint Francis of Sales (1567–1622) addressed the teachings of his work *Introduction to the Devout Life* to Philothea, whose names means "lover of God."

character. Devotion must be practiced in a different way by the gentleman, by the workman, by the servant, by the prince, by the widow, by the unmarried woman and the married one. That is not sufficient, but the practice of devotion must also be adapted to the strength, the employment, and the duties of each one in particular. . . . It is an error, or rather a heresy, to try to banish the devout life from the regiment of soldiers, the mechanics' workshop, the court of princes, or the homes of married people. It is true, Philothea, that a purely contemplative, monastic, and religious devotion cannot be exercised in those states, but, besides these three types of devotion, there are several others adapted to bring perfection to those who live in the secular state. Therefore, wherever we are, we can and should aspire to the perfect life."

Along the same lines, the Second Vatican Council states: *"This lay spirituality should take its particular character from the circumstances of one's state in life (married and family life, celibacy, or widowhood), from one's state of health, and from one's professional and social activity. All must not cease to cultivate the qualities and talents bestowed on them in accord with those conditions, and should make use of the gifts they have received from the Holy Spirit."*

What is valid for spiritual vocations is also valid, and in a certain sense with greater reason, for the infinite ways in which all the members of the Church are laborers in the vineyard of the Lord, building up the mystical body of Christ. Truly each one, with his unique and singular personal history, is called by name, to bring his own contribution to the coming of the Kingdom of God. No talent, no matter how small, is to be hidden or left unutilized.

In this regard, the Apostle Peter gives us a stern warning: *"As each has received a gift, employ it for one another, as good stewards of God's varied grace."*

CHRISTIFIDELES LAICI, 56

The transparency of Christ

You must make Christ present by unreservedly welcoming the radical spirit of the beatitudes, aware that the consecrated life is "a privileged means for effective evangelization."

A sense of participation in the life of the Church will be fostered in those who are integrated into various activities and comforted by prayer. It is good to observe your growing conviction that you are members of God's people with a special vocation to consecration. It is good to see in you the Church as the virgin who awaits her bridegroom with the lighted lamp, a light for others and living witness of the values of the Kingdom.

This desire to be the transparency of Christ for others places you in a position of great importance and dignity, as men and women consecrated in the Church for the good of all humanity. Your duties have a profound ecclesiastical and social impact, since you can offer something of your own, that is, the gifts of a rich spirituality and a vast capacity for disinterested love. From the perspective of your integration into the Church, I encourage you to rejoice in your special presence, in full and faithful communion with the hierarchy, since there cannot be a genuine integration into the Church outside of the center of communion, which is the bishop in his diocese. Thus you will be the true light, the light of Christ in his Church, light that radiates its own self-fulfillment.

PARAGUAY, MAY 17, 1988

Through the initiative of the Savior and your generous response, *Christ* has become *the purpose of your existence and the center of all your thoughts.* For Christ you have professed the evangelical counsels; and Christ will sustain you in full faithfulness to Him and in loving service to his Church.

Religious consecration is essentially *an act of love:* the love of Christ for you and, in return, your love for him and for all his brothers and sisters. This mystery is proclaimed today in the Gospel when Jesus says to his disciples: *"As the Father has loved me, so have I loved you; abide in my love."* Christ wants you to abide in him, by being nourished by him daily in the celebration of the Eucharist and by giving your life back to him through prayer and self-denial. Trusting in his word and putting faith in his mercy, you respond to his love; you choose to follow him more nearly in chastity, poverty, and obedience, with the desire to participate more fully in the life and holiness of the Church. You wish to love as brothers and sisters all those whom Christ loves.

PHILIPPINES, FEBRUARY 17, 1981

More than ever, our world needs to discover, in your communities and your way of life, the value of a simple life in the service of the poor. It needs to know the value of a life freely pledged to *celibacy* to preserve itself for Christ and, with him, to love especially the unloved. It needs to know the value of a life in which obedience and fraternal community silently challenge the excesses of an independence that is sometimes capricious and sterile.

Above all, the world needs testimony of the *generosity of God's love*. Among those who doubt God or believe that he is absent, you are the demonstration that it is worthwhile to seek the Lord and love him for himself, that it is worthwhile to consecrate one's life to the Kingdom of God, and its apparent foolishness. Your lives thus become a sign of the indestructible faith of the Church. The free gift of one's life to Christ and to others is perhaps the most pressing challenge to a society in which money has become an idol. Your choice confounds, raises questions, lures, or annoys this world, but never leaves it indifferent. The Gospel is always, and in every way, a sign of contradiction.

> But *never be afraid to demonstrate*
> *your devotion to the Lord.*
> It does honor to you!
> It honors the Church!
> You have a specific place in the body of Christ,
> in which each of you must fulfill
> his own task,
> his own charism.

If, with the Holy Spirit, you seek the *holiness* that corresponds to your state of life, have no fear. He will not abandon you. Vocations will come to you.

And you yourselves will preserve your youthfulness of spirit, which has nothing to do with age. Yes, live in hope. Keep your eyes fixed on Christ and walk firmly in his footsteps, in joy and peace.

CANADA, SEPTEMBER 19, 1984

"If you keep my commandments, you will abide in my love." Faith is the proof of love. In addition, Christians have the right to require of a consecrated person sincere adherence and obedience to the commandments of Christ and his Church. Therefore, you must avoid everything that might make people think that the Church maintains a dual hierarchy or a dual Magisterium.* Always live and instill profound love for the Church, and loyal adherence to all its teachings. Convey certainties of faith, not uncertainties. Always communicate the truths that the Magisterium states, not ideologies that come and go. To build up the Church, live holiness. It will lead you, if necessary, to the supreme test of love for others, because *"greater love has no man than this, that a man lay down his life for his friends."*

Along these lines, I wish to express all my respect and encouragement for the members of Secular Institutes and Associations of Apostolic Life, who work actively and give testimony of Christ, by their special presence, in all areas of Church life.

PERU, FEBRUARY 1, 1985

---

* The Magisterium is the teaching office of the Church, whose task it is to give an authentic interpretation of the word of God, whether in its written form or in the form of tradition.

You are called on to take up your role in the evangelization of the world. Yes, the laity are *"a chosen people, a holy priesthood."* They are called on to be *"the salt of the earth"* and *"the light of the world."* It is their vocation and their unique mission to manifest the Gospel in their lives and also to add it as leaven to the world in which they live and work. The great forces that rule the world—politics, mass media, science, technology, culture, education, industry, and work—represent precisely the areas in which lay people are competent to carry out their mission. If these forces are controlled by people who are true disciples of Christ and whose knowledge and talents make them, at the same time, experts in their particular field, then the world will truly be changed from within by the redeeming power of Christ.

AUGUST 28, 1980

Be witnesses!

I would like to urge you today: *Be witnesses*. Witnesses of the hope that is rooted in faith. Witnesses of the invisible in a secularized society, which too often ignores every transcendent dimension.

Yes, consecrated souls: among the people of this generation, who are so immersed in the *relative*, you must be voices that speak of the *absolute*. Perhaps you have, so to speak, thrown all your resources into the scales of the world, gladly tipping them toward God and the goods promised by him? You have made a decisive choice about your life: you have opted for generosity and giving in the face of greed and self-interest; you have chosen to count on love and grace, challenging those who consider you ingenuous and ineffectual; you have placed every hope on the Kingdom of Heaven, when many around you are striving only to assure for themselves a comfortable stay on earth.

It is up to you, now, to *be integrated,* in spite of every difficulty. The spiritual destiny of many souls is linked to your faith and your integration.

You must be the constant reminder of that destiny which unfolds in time but has eternity as its goal, bearing witness with our words, and even more with your lives, that we must of necessity direct ourselves toward the one who is the inescapable end point of the parabola of our existence.

> Your vocation
> makes you the advance guard
> of mankind on the march:
> in your prayers
> and in your work,
> in your joy
> and in your suffering,
> in your successes

and in your trials,
mankind must be able to find
the model and the future
of what it, too,
is called to be,
in spite of its own burdens
and its own compromises.

BOLOGNA, APRIL 18, 1982

The world needs your testimony

The world today needs to see your love for Christ; it needs public testimony of the religious life: as Paul VI once said: *"Modern man listens more willingly to witnesses than to teachers, and if he listens to teachers he does so because they are witnesses."* If the nonbelievers of this world are to believe in Christ, they need your faithful testimony—testimony that springs from your complete trust in the generous mercy of the Father and in your enduring faith in the power of the cross and the resurrection. Thus the ideals, the values, the convictions that are the basis of your dedication to Christ must be translated into the language of daily life. Among the people of God, in the local ecclesial community, your public testimony is part of your contribution to the mission of the Church. As St. Paul says: *"You are a letter from Christ . . . written not with ink but with the Spirit of the living God, not on tablets of stone but on tablets of human hearts."*

PHILIPPINES, FEBRUARY 17, 1981

Taking an interest in the world in order to transform it

Christians, and especially you members of the laity, are called by God to become interested in the world in order to transform it according to the Gospel. Your personal commitment to truth and honesty occupies an important position in the fulfillment of that task, because a sense of responsibility to truth constitutes one of the fundamental meeting points between the Church and society, between the Church and each man or woman. The Christian faith does not provide ready-made solutions to the complex problems of contemporary society, but it does provide a deep understanding of human nature and its needs, calling you to tell the truth in charity, to take up your responsibilities as good citizens, and to work, along with your neighbor, to construct a society in which genuine human values are fostered and intensified through a shared Christian vision of life.

NAIROBI, MAY 7, 1980

We have to be for others

Our times require mature and balanced personalities.

Ideological confusion produces psychologically immature and needy personalities; pedagogy itself wavers and sometimes goes astray. For this very reason, the modern world searches anxiously for models, and most of the time remains disappointed, defeated, humiliated. That is why we have to develop mature personalities, which means learning to keep our selfishness in check, assuming our proper roles of responsibility and leadership, and trying to fulfill ourselves wherever we are and in whatever work we do.

Our times require serenity and courage to accept reality as it is, without discouraging criticisms or utopian fantasies, to love it and to save it.

All of you, then, undertake to reach these ideals of "maturity," through love of duty, meditation, spiritual reading, examination of your conscience, spiritual guidance, and regular use of the Sacrament of Repentance. The Church and modern society need mature personalities: we must fill that need, with the help of God!

Finally, our times require a serious commitment to holiness.

The spiritual needs of the present world are immense! It is almost frightening to look at the infinite forests of buildings in a modern metropolis, inhabited by countless numbers of people. How will we be able to reach all these people and lead them to Christ?

The certainty that we are merely instruments of grace comes to our aid: acting in the individual soul is God himself, with his love and mercy.

Our true, lifelong commitment must be to personal sanctification, so that we may be fit and efficacious instruments of grace.

The truest and most sincere wish I have for you is just this: "Become holy and soon be saints!"

ST. PIO V PARISH, OCTOBER 28, 1979

If you have met Christ,
proclaim it in the first person

If you have met Christ, live Christ, live with Christ! Proclaim it in the first person, as genuine testimony: *"For me life is Christ."* That is true liberation: to proclaim Jesus free of ties, present in men and women, transformed, made new creatures. Why instead at times does our testimony seem to be in vain? Because we present Jesus without the full seductive power of his person, without revealing the treasures of the sublime ideal inherent in following him; and because we are not always successful in demonstrating conviction, translated into living terms, regarding the extraordinary value of the gift of ourselves to the ecclesial cause we serve.

Brothers and sisters: it is important that men see in us dispensers of the mysteries of God, credible witnesses of his presence in the world. We frequently remember that God, when he calls us, asks for not only one part of our person but all our person and all our vital energies, so that we may announce to men the joy and peace of a new life in Christ, and guide them to a meeting with him. So let it be our first concern to seek the Lord, and, once we have met him, to observe where and how he lives, by being with him all day. Being with him, in a special way, in the Eucharist, where Christ gives himself to us; and in prayer, through which we give ourselves to him. The Eucharist must be performed and extended into our daily actions as a "sacrifice of praise." In prayer, in the trusting contact with God our Father, we can discern better where our strengths and weaknesses are, because the Spirit comes to our aid. The same Spirit speaks to us and slowly immerses us in the divine mysteries, in God's design of love for humanity, which he realizes through our willingness to serve him.

JANUARY 26, 1979

45

Dear friends, I invite you above all to *give thanks to God*. He offers you an extraordinary gift in calling you to leave everything to follow him and serve him. This call can be heard in many ways: it becomes part of each one's secret history; the Church affirmed it. Preserve the memory of the Lord's blessings, and walk in hope. The gifts of the Lord are without repentance. On this path you, like Christ, like Mary, will obviously find your cross. You suffer because of the obstacles that the Gospel encounters, when your mission is to preach to the world; you suffer also from your labors, your limits, sometimes from your weaknesses. *Be content* to be so close to Christ and so useful to the Church. Even if, often, you cannot visibly check the results of your ministry, rejoice, as Jesus said to his apostles, in the fact that your names are written in Heaven. If you are faithful, you will always find Christ's peace.

You know the path of faith. Put prayer at the center of your lives. Live in close union with Christ. Live with him all the encounters and activities of your apostolate. Remain united among yourselves, so that none of you will lack fraternal support.

BELGIUM, MAY 18, 1985

"Be of good cheer," Jesus says to you, *"I have overcome the world."*

If Jesus asks you for faith, it is because he gave you faith first, he gave you faith when, with an absolutely free gesture of love, he called you to follow him more nearly, to *"leave house or brothers or sisters or mother or father or lands for my sake and the Gospel."* He gave you faith when, with a special outpouring of the Spirit, he consecrated you and, amid the diversity of gifts and ministries, *"chose you and appointed you that you should go and bear fruit and that your fruit should abide."* He gave you faith when he chose you and sent you—you precisely—to be heralds of his Kingdom, witnesses of his Resurrection, a prophetic sign of the *"new heavens and a new earth, in which righteousness dwells."*

Your mission, like the mission of the entire Church at the end of the second Christian millennium, is not easy.

Jesus did not hide from his Apostles the *difficulties of the mission:* the rejection, the hostility, the persecution they would encounter. *"If the world hates you, know that it has hated me before it hated you.... Remember the word that I said to you: A servant is not greater than his master. If they persecuted me, they will persecute you, too."*

That which might seem an obstacle to your mission becomes, in the light of faith, the secret of its fruitfulness. The presence of the paschal Christ assures us that, just when we seem defeated, then we are the conquerors, in fact "more than conquerors." It is the remarkable logic that flows from the Cross. On the human level, the Cross of Jesus is a notable failure; but from it derives the explosive newness that changed the face of life and human history.

Here is the secret of our faith: when we are weak, it is then that we are strong; and the weaker we are, the stronger we are, because the more we let the presence and the power of the paschal Christ shine through. And with this paradox the Church has walked for two thousand years already and will go on walking . . . nothing else, only this paradox.

The Spirit of God is the Spirit of life, which can make life explode even where everything seemed dead and parched. That is why we can and must have faith. We not only can but must. Hope for Christians, and even more for the consecrated, is not a luxury, it is a duty. To hope is not to dream; on the contrary, it is to let oneself be seized by he who can transform the dream into reality.

REGGIO EMILIA, JUNE 6, 1988

Strive to be witnesses of Christ's love by putting into practice his Word of Life.

When you help your neighbor, whoever he is, you proclaim the Good News of Christ, which makes universal brotherhood possible.

When you visit a sick person, you are a sign of Christ's mercy toward those who suffer.

When you forgive, even your worst enemy, you are a sign of the forgiveness of Christ, who never nourished hatred in his heart.

When you refuse to accuse someone without proof, you proclaim the coming of the Kingdom of God and his justice, and no one is excluded.

When, as Christian spouses, you remain faithful in marriage, you are an encouragement to all and a sign of the eternal covenant of love between God and man.

When, as a young man or a young woman, you save yourself for the one who will be your spouse, you are testimony of the unique value that love can construct.

When you radiate Christ, you awaken a desire for total self-giving in his service and inspire new priestly and religious vocations.

When, in the light, you call evil that which is evil and refuse to practice it, you are witnesses of Christ's Light.

May our Lord of Peace help you to be, for your brothers and sisters, men and women of light, authors of peace and reconciliation who can be builders of a more just and fraternal world.

CHAD, JUNE 30, 1990

You must be *the sign and leaven of brotherhood*. God wishes to build in the world the great family of God, where all men, of every race, color and condition, can live together in a spirit of fellowship and peace. You are already a wonderful manifestation of this family. Therefore you can help your people establish themselves as a people-family, from different families and cultures. . . .

Finally, you must be *the sign and leaven of the liberating and saving Love of God for your people and for all men*. Consecrated love originates in the Holy Spirit, but as a response to situations and needs in the Church and in men. God is the Savior and does not want anyone to be lost.

All those who approach you would like to see the face of Christ the Redeemer, *"who desires all men to be saved and to come to the knowledge of the truth."* Be witnesses of God in your way of life and prayer, open up *"the immense spaces of charity, of the evangelical proclamation, of Christian education, of culture, and of solidarity with the poor, the discriminated against, the marginalized, and the oppressed."* Be the vehicle of liberating hope for those who suffer because of slavery, and lead your brothers and sisters to the Sacrament of divine Mercy, of Reconciliation.

Be a sign of God. You must be his witnesses: he is the center and the source of life for mankind.

ANGOLA, JUNE 9, 1992

The Church would like to thank the Most Holy Trinity for the "mystery of woman," and, for every woman—for what constitutes the eternal measure of her feminine dignity, for the "great works of God" which throughout human history have been accomplished in her and through her. After all, wasn't the greatest event in human history—the incarnation of God himself—accomplished in her and through her?

The Church, therefore, *gives thanks for each and every woman:* for mothers, for sisters, for wives; for women consecrated to God in virginity; for women dedicated to the many human beings who await the freely given love of another person; for women who watch over the human beings in the family, which is the fundamental sign of the human community; for women who work professionally, and who are at times burdened by a great social responsibility; for *"perfect"* women and for "weak" women—for all women as they have come forth from the heart of God in all the beauty and richness of their femininity; as they have been embraced by his eternal love; as, together with men, they are pilgrims on this earth, which is the temporal "homeland" of mankind and is sometimes transformed into a "vale of tears"; as they take on, together with men, a common responsibility for the destiny of humanity, according to daily necessities and according to that definitive destiny which the human family has in God himself, in the bosom of the ineffable Trinity.

The Church gives thanks *for all the manifestations of feminine "genius"* that have appeared in the course of history, amid all peoples and nations; she gives thanks for all the charisms that the Holy Spirit has distributed to women in the history of the people of God, for all the victories that the Church owes to their faith, hope, and charity: she gives thanks for all the fruits of feminine holiness.

The Church asks, at the same time, that these invaluable "manifestations of the Spirit" which are generously poured forth on the "daughters" of eternal Jerusalem be attentively recognized and appreciated, so that they may return to the common benefit of the Church and humanity, especially in our times. Pondering the Biblical mystery of "woman," the Church prays that all women may discover in this mystery themselves and their "supreme vocation."

MULIERIS DIGNITATEM, 31

Being with Jesus

How is it possible for a consecrated person, fully taken up with apostolic activity, to grow in his inner life without equal periods of prayer and worship?

Silence is vital space devoted to the Lord, in an atmosphere of listening to his word and assimilating it; it is a sanctuary of prayer, the hearth of reflection and contemplation. To remain fervent and zealous in one's ministry, one must be able to receive divine inspiration from within. And that is possible only if one is capable of *being* with the divine Teacher. Jesus did not call the Twelve only to *"send them forth to preach and to have power to heal sickness and to cast out devils"* but, above all, so that *"they should be with him."*

Being with Jesus: let this be your greatest desire. Be with him as the Apostles were and, earlier, in Nazareth, Mary and Joseph. Speak to him in an intimate way, listen to him, follow him docilely: this is not only a comprehensible requirement for those who want to follow the Lord; it is also an indispensable condition of all authentic and credible evangelization. He is an empty preacher of the Word — St. Augustine aptly observes — who does not first listen to it within himself.

Be united with Christ forever. The methods that the millenarian wisdom of the Church is never tired of recommending to the faithful, so that they may be disposed to supernatural grace — frequent practice of the Sacrament of Repentance, devout participation in the Holy Mass, celebration of the Liturgy of the Hours, the *Lectio Divina,* Eucharistic worship, the Spiritual Exercises, reciting the Rosary — should be sought and cherished by you, dear brothers and sisters, with even more reason, for you are more closely united with the mission of the Redeemer.

Before being organizers of your communities, be models of prayer and spiritual perfection for them. By constant recourse to prayer you will be able to draw on the inner strength necessary to overcome difficulties, conquer temptations, and grow in charity and fidelity to your vocation.

SORRENTO, MARCH 19, 1992

53

I conclude by encouraging you to be men and women of *prayer,* because the Spirit of God must be the soul of your apostolate, permeate your thoughts, your desires, your actions, purify them, elevate them. Like priests and religious, lay people are called to holiness; prayer is the honored pathway. And then you have many occasions to thank and intercede for all those you are close to. I learn with great pleasure that there has been a true revival of prayer, which translates into, among other things, a flowering of prayer groups, but which also, I hope, informs the life of your movements. God be praised! May the Virgin Mary always accompany the apostolate that you perform in the name of her Son. And, in expressing my trust and joy, I bless you, along with the members of your movements and your friends and families, from the bottom of my heart.

FRANCE, MAY 31, 1980

The Virgin continues to be the model for every consecrated person. She is the consecrated woman, the Virgin of Nazareth, who, listening, praying, and loving, was chosen to be the Mother of God. *"If the entire Church finds in Mary its primary model, you who are consecrated people and communities within the Church have even more reason to do so."*

Humble and forgetful of herself, Mary dedicated her life so that the will of the Lord might be fulfilled in her. Her life was placed in the service of God's plan for salvation.

She was truly happy and fortunate. Deprived of every power that did not come from the force of the Spirit that overshadowed her, she did not avoid the cross but lived in conjugal faithfulness to the Lord as a model and Mother of the Church.

May the Virgin accompany you always; may she teach you the path of faith and humble joy that comes of putting your existence in the service of the Kingdom; may she guide you and encourage you on the path of holiness and in your evangelical activities.

On this occasion I wish to address a special word of encouragement to the members of the Secular Institutes, who, with their style of consecrated life, affirmed by the Second Vatican Council, perform an extremely important service in the Church, responding to new apostolic challenges and being themselves the leaven of Christ in the world.

Your charism represents service of great value in today's world. Your apostolic activities glorify God and contribute effectively to the achievement of that civilization of love that is the divine plan for humanity, which awaits its glorious coming.

CHILE, APRIL 3, 1987

O Mary,
Mother of Mercy,
watch over all people
so that Christ's cross was not in vain,
so that man does not stray from the path of the good,
or become blind to sin,
but so that he puts his hope ever more more fully in God
who is "rich in mercy."
May he carry out generously the good works
prepared by God beforehand,
and so live completely
"in praise of his glory."

VERITATIS SPLENDOR

The era of missions is not over

The era of missions is not over;
Christ still needs
generous men and women
who will become messengers
of the Good News
to the ends of the earth.
Have no fear of following him.
Share freely with others
the faith that you have received!
"No believer in Christ,
no institution of the Church
can be separate from this supreme duty:
proclaiming Christ to all the people."

GAMBIA, FEBRUARY 23, 1992

From
An Invitation to Prayer

The Church exists for prayer

I would like to speak to you about the *call to prayer*.

We have meditated on these words of Jesus: *"Pray that you may have strength . . . to stand before the Son of man."* And we welcome again today the call to prayer that comes from Christ himself to each of us and to the whole Church. *The call to prayer places the Church's full commitment in the proper perspective.* In 1976, Paul VI, speaking of the "call to commitment," declared that *"in the tradition of the Church every call to action is first of all a call to prayer."* These words have great significance today, too. They are a stimulus for the Church everywhere in the world.

The universal Church of Christ, and hence every particular church, *exists for prayer*. In prayer the individual expresses his nature; the community expresses its vocation; the Church approaches God. In prayer the Church enters into communion with the Father and with his Son, Jesus Christ. *In prayer the Church expresses her Trinitarian life,* because it is directed to the Father, is subjected to the action of the Holy Spirit, and lives fully the relationship with Christ. Indeed, *it is experienced* as the Body of Christ, as mystical Christ.

The Church encounters Christ in prayer in the depths of her being. In this way she discovers the truth of his teachings and assumes his mentality. Seeking to live a personal relationship with Christ, the Church fully realizes the personal dignity of her members. In prayer the Church focuses on Christ; she takes Christ; she takes possession of him, she tastes his friendship, and thus is able to communicate it. Without prayer, all this would be lacking and the Church would have nothing to offer the world. But through the exercise of faith, hope, and charity in prayer, her capacity to communicate Christ is strengthened.

Prayer *is the objective of every catechesis* in the Church, since it is a means of union with God. Through prayer the Church expresses the authority of God and fulfills the first and great commandment of love.

Every aspect of human existence is marked by prayer. *Man's work is revolutionized by prayer,* raised to its highest level. Prayer is the means by which work is fully humanized. In prayer the value of work is understood, because we grasp the fact that we are truly collaborators with God in the action of transforming and elevating the world. Prayer consecrates this collaboration. At the same time prayer is a way of confronting the problems of life, and in prayer every pastoral undertaking is conceived and carried forward.

The call to prayer must precede the call to action, but the call to action must in fact accompany the call to prayer. *The Church finds in prayer the root of social commitment*—the capacity to motivate and sustain it. In prayer we discover the needs of our brothers and sisters and make them our needs, because in prayer we discover that their needs are the needs of Christ. *Social consciousness is formed by prayer.* According to the words of Jesus, justice and mercy are the "weightier matters of the law." The Church's commitment to justice and her search for mercy will be successful only if the Holy Spirit gives the gift of perseverance: this gift must be sought in prayer.

In prayer we arrive at an understanding of the beatitudes and the reasons for living them. Only through prayer can we begin to see the aspirations of men according to the perspective of Christ. Without the intuitions of prayer we would never be able to grasp *all the dimensions of human development* and the urgency, for the Christian community, of commitment to this work.

Prayer invites us to examine our consciences with regard to all the problems that afflict humanity. It invites us to evaluate our responsibilities, personal and collective, before God's judgment and in the light of human solidarity. For this reason, prayer transforms the world. Everything is renewed, both in individuals and in communities. *New goals and new ideals emerge.* Dignity and Christian action are reaffirmed. The promises of baptism, confirmation, and Holy Orders acquire new urgency. Prayer opens up the horizons of conjugal love and of the mission of the family.

Christian sensibility depends on prayer. Prayer is the essential condition—even if not the only one—*for a correct reading of the "signs of the times."* Without prayer we are inevitably deceived on this delicate subject.

Decisions require prayer; major decisions require intense prayer. Jesus himself gave us the example. Before calling together the disciples so that he could choose twelve of them, Jesus spent the night on the mountain, in communion with the Father. For Jesus, praying to the Father did not mean only light and strength. It meant also trust, abandonment, and joy. His human nature exulted in the joy of prayer. In every age, the intensity of the Church's joy is proportionate to her prayer.

The strength of her authority and the condition for her confidence are fidelity to prayer. The mysteries of Christ are revealed to those who approach him in prayer. The full application of the Second Vatican Council will always be conditional on prayer. The great strides made by lay people in the Church in understanding how much they belong to the Church can be explained, in the final analysis, only by grace and its acceptance in prayer.

In the life of the Church today we often notice that *the gift of prayer is joined to the Word of God.* A renewed discovery of the Sacred Scriptures has developed the fruits of prayer. The word of God, accepted and meditated on, has the power to bring our hearts into closer communion with the Holy Trinity. This happens more and more in the Church of today. The benefits we receive through prayer that is joined to the Word of God impel us to respond with more prayers (prayers of praise and thanksgiving).

The Word of God generates prayer in all communities. At the same time it is in prayer that the Word of God is understood, applied, and lived. For all of us who are ministers of the Gospel, with the pastoral responsibility to announce the Good News *opportune et importune*—in season and out of season—and to carefully examine the reality of daily life in the light of the sacred Word of God, prayer is the context in which we prepare the declaration of faith. *All evangelization is prepared for in prayer;* in prayer first of all it applies to ourselves; in prayer it is then offered to the world.

Every local church is truly itself in the degree to which it is a community of prayer, with all the resulting dynamism that prayer effects. The universal Church is never so much herself as when she reflects faithfully the image of Christ in prayer: the Son who, praying, turns his entire being to the Father and consecrates himself for love of his brothers, *"that they also may be consecrated in truth."*

For this reason, dear brothers in the Episcopate, I wish to encourage you in all your efforts *to teach people to pray.* It is the job of the Apostolic Church to transmit the teachings of Jesus to all the generations, to offer faithfully to every local church the response of Jesus to the request: *"Teach us to pray."* I assure you of my support and that of the whole Church in your commitment *to preach the importance of daily prayer and give the example of prayer.* From the words of Jesus we know that wherever two or three are gathered in his name, he is among them. And we know that in every local church gathered in prayer around the bishop lives the incomparable beauty of the entire Catholic Church as the faithful image of Christ in prayer.

In his task as pastor of the universal Church, the successor of Peter is called on to live a communion of prayer with his brother bishops and their dioceses, and for this reason all your initiatives to promote prayer have my full support. In fraternal and pastoral charity I am near you when you call your people to daily prayer, when you invite them to discover in prayer their dignity as Christians. *Every diocesan or parish initiative* that exhorts us to more intense prayer, on the part of both individuals and families, is a blessing for the universal Church. Every group that gathers to recite the Rosary is a gift for the Kingdom of God. Yes, wherever two or three are gathered in the name of Christ, he is there. The contemplative communities are a special gift of God's love for his people. They need and deserve the fullness of your love and pastoral support. Their particular job in the world is to testify to the supremacy of God and the primacy of Christ's love, *"which surpasses all understanding."*

Profoundly convinced of the power of prayer and humbly engaged in it, dear brothers, we confidently proclaim throughout the whole Church the call to prayer. At stake is the very necessity for the Church to be herself, the Church at prayer, for the glory of the Father. The Holy Spirit will assist us and the merits of the Paschal Mystery of Christ will make up for our human weakness.

The example of Mary, the Mother of Jesus, as the model of prayer, is a source of confident trust for all of us. Looking at her, we are aware that her example sustains our priests, religious, and lay people. We know that her generosity is an inheritance for the whole Church to proclaim and imitate.

To a group of American bishops
on a visit *"ad limina,"*[*]
June 10, 1988

---

[*] The visit *ad limina* means, technically, the obligation incumbent on the bishops of visiting, at stated times, the "thresholds of the Apostles," Sts. Peter and Paul, and of presenting themselves before the Pope to give an account of the state of their dioceses.

Why pray?

We must "always pray and not lose heart."

Why must we pray?

We must pray first of all because we are believers.

Prayer is in fact the recognition of our limits and our dependence: we come from God, we are of God, and to God we return! We can therefore only abandon ourselves to him, our Lord and Creator, with absolute, total trust.

Prayer is first of all an act of intelligence, a feeling of humility and gratefulness, an attitude of trust and abandonment to the one who gave us his life for love.

Prayer is a mysterious but real dialogue with God, a dialogue of confidence and love.

We are, however, Christians, and so we must pray as Christians.

In fact, for the Christian prayer acquires a special character, which changes its intimate nature and its intimate value.

The Christian is a disciple of Jesus; he believes truly that Jesus is the Word Incarnate; the Son of God come among us on this earth.

Therefore, the Christian knows that his prayer is Jesus; every one of his prayers starts from Jesus; it is he who prays in us, with us, for us.

All those who believe in God pray; but the Christian prays in Jesus Christ: Christ is our prayer!

The greatest prayer is the Holy Mass, because in the Holy Mass Jesus himself is fully present, as he renews the sacrifice of the Cross; but every prayer is valid, especially the Our Father, which he himself wished to teach the Apostles and all men on earth.

Saying the words of the Our Father, Jesus created a specific and, at the same time, universal model. Indeed, all that we can and must say to the Father is contained in those seven requests, which we all know by heart. They are so simple that even a child can learn them, but at the same time so profound that one can spend a lifetime meditating on their meaning.

Finally, we must continue to pray because we are frail and full of guilt.

We must recognize humbly and realistically that we are poor creatures, confused in our ideas, tempted to evil, frail and weak, continually in need of inner strength and comfort.

— Prayer gives us the strength for grand ideals, the strength to maintain our faith, charity, purity, generosity;
— Prayer gives us the courage to emerge from indifference and sin if, unfortunately, we have yielded to temptation and weakness;
— Prayer gives us light by which to see and to consider the events of our own life and of history itself in the salvific perspective of God and eternity.

Therefore, do not stop praying! Do not let a day pass without praying a little! Prayer is a duty, but it is also a great joy, because it is a dialogue with God through Jesus Christ.

Celebrate the Holy Mass every Sunday, and if possible sometimes during the week as well; every day say prayers in the morning and evening and at any other opportune moments!

MARCH 14, 1979

Family prayer

The family has always been at the center of ecclesial attention.

If we ask the "why" of such interest, it is not difficult to find it in the *love and service that the Church owes man*. Christianity is the religion of the Incarnation, it is the joyous proclamation of a God who comes to meet man and becomes man.

For this reason, ever since my first encyclical, I have not hesitated to affirm that man is the *"Way of the Church,"* intending by that to recall and as it were retrace the road traversed by God himself, when, through the Incarnation and the Redemption, he set off on the path of his creation.

But how to meet man, without meeting the family? Man is essentially a "social" being; more accurately, one could say a *"family"* being. The family is the natural place of his coming into the world, it is the environment in which normally he receives what he needs in order to develop, it is the primordial emotional nucleus that gives him coherence and confidence, it is the first school of social relations.

We can say: here is "the Gospel of the family," which the Church intends to present with renewed energy. This year, which the Lord offers to us, will be testimony and proclamation, a time of reflection and a time of conversion: *a time of special prayer,* prayer *for* families, prayer *in* families, prayer *of* families.

It is time to discover the value of prayer, its mysterious force, its capacity not only to lead us back to God but to introduce us to the *radical truth of the human being*.

When a person prays, he places himself before God, a you, a divine you, and at the same time grasps the inmost truth of his own "I": You the divine, I the human, the personal being created in the image of God.

This occurs similarly in *family prayer*: placing itself in the light of the Lord, the family feels that it is profoundly a *communal subject*, a "we" cemented by an eternal design of love, that nothing in the world can destroy.

We look at Mary, the Bride and the Mother of the Family of Nazareth. She is a living icon of prayer, *in a family of prayer*. Precisely for this reason she is also the image of serenity and peace, of giving and faith, of tenderness and hope. And what she is, every family must be, too.

> Holy Virgin, we ask you
> to teach us to pray.
> We ask of you
> the great gift of love
> in all the families of the world.
>
> ANGELUS, JANUARY 30, 1994

To God the Creator

God, you are our Creator.
You are good
and your mercy is infinite.
God, you have given to us men
an inner law
that we must live by.
To do your will
and accomplish our task.
To follow your paths
and know peace in our soul.
To you we offer our obedience.
Guide us in all the initiatives
that we undertake on earth.
Free us from our evil tendencies,
which turn our hearts away
from your will.
Do not allow
us to invoke your name
to justify human strife.
O God, you are the one and only.
You we adore.
Do not let us distance ourselves from you.
God, judge of all men,
help us to be among the chosen
on the last day.
God, author of justice and peace,
grant us true joy,
and genuine love,
and enduring brotherhood
among peoples.
Fill us with your eternal gifts.
Amen!

AUGUST 19, 1985

"Though he was rich, he became poor"

We give thanks to you, O Our Father, for the Word that became flesh and, on that night in Bethlehem, came to live among us.

We thank you for the Word, with which you communicate for eternity the holy reality of your divinity.

We thank you for the Word, in which before the beginning of time you decided to create the world, so that it might bear witness to you.

We thank you, because in your Word *you loved man* "before the foundation of the world."

We thank you, because in him, your chosen Son, you decided to *renew all creation; you decided to redeem man.*

We thank you, eternal Father, for the night in Bethlehem when God was born, when the Word became flesh and the *power of Redemption* came to live among us.

We thank you for the *inheritance of your grace,* which you have not taken from the heart of man but have renewed through the earthly birth of your Son, so that we, by means of his Cross and his Resurrection, could regain, from generation to generation, the *dignity of children of God,* which was lost through sin, the dignity of adopted brothers of your eternal Son. We give thanks to you, O Holy Father, for your *holy name,* which you have allowed to flower in our hearts through the Redemption of the world.

We thank you, eternal Father, for the *motherhood of the Virgin Mary,* who under the protection of Joseph, the carpenter of Nazareth, brought your Son into the world, in poverty.

We thank you, Heavenly Father, for the Child laid in a manger: in him "the goodness and loving kindness of God our Savior appeared."

We thank you, eternal Father, *for this love,* which comes *like a feeble infant into the story of each man.*

We thank you, because, "though he was rich, he became poor for us, so that we might become rich by means of his poverty."

We thank you for the marvelous *economy of the Redemption* of man and the world, which was revealed for the first time on the night of the birth in Bethlehem.

Our Father!

Look with the eyes of the newborn Child at men who are dying of hunger, while huge sums are committed to weapons. Look at the unspeakable grief of parents who must witness the agony of their children who beg them for bread that they do not have, and that could be procured with even a tiny fraction of the lavish amounts being spent on sophisticated means of destruction, because of which, the clouds that gather on the horizon of humanity become more and more threatening.

Hear, O Father, the cry for peace that rises from populations martyred by war, and speak to the hearts of those who can help to find, through negotiations and dialogue, fair and honorable solutions to the ongoing conflicts.

Look at the anxious and tormented road of so many people who are struggling to find the means of survival, to advance and raise themselves.

Look at the pain and anguish that lacerate the souls of those who are forced to live far from their families or who live in families torn apart by selfishness and infidelity; of those who are without work, without a home, without a country, without love, without hope.

Look at the peoples who are without joy and security, because they see their fundamental rights violated; look at our world of today, with its hopes and its disappointments, with its courage and its cowardice, with its noble ideals and its humiliating compromises.

Urge individuals and peoples to break down the wall of selfishness, of aggression and hatred, to open themselves to fraternal respect toward every individual, near and far, because we are all human, because we are brothers and sisters in Christ.

Enable each of us to bring the necessary aid to those who are in need, to give ourselves for the good of all, to renew our hearts in the grace of Christ the Redeemer.

Help your Church to do its utmost for the poor, for the dispossessed, for the suffering.

Preserve and strengthen in all hearts the yearning for faith in you and kindness toward our brothers; the search for your presence and your love; trust in your redeeming power, confidence in your forgiveness, and abandonment to your Providence.

Jesus Christ, the Son of the living God, born that night in Bethlehem to the Virgin Mary! Jesus Christ, our brother and our Redeemer! With your first look, embrace the troubles that assail the world of today! Born on the earth, receive into your communion all the peoples and nations of the earth.

Receive us all, men and women, your brothers and sisters who are in need of your love and your mercy.

DECEMBER 25, 1983

God of our daily work

"You are blessed, God of the universe." *Yes, blessed are you, Lord, God of our families!* God of our daily work. God of our joys and of our sorrows!

We pray to you for all those who suffer, for those who have no money, those who have no education, those who are in need of affection: make us attentive to their wants and teach us to share.

We pray to you for the unemployed and for young people who are looking for work: help us to prepare a place for them in our society.

We pray to you for the sick, for those who have lost all hope of getting well, for those who are nearing death: sustain them, comfort them, console them, give them patience and serenity.

We pray to you for those in this nation who are hungry, for those who are exiled, for refugees. Lord, master of the impossible, put an end to our sorrows, expand our hearts, and bring us together in unity.

Finally, *we pray to you and glorify you* for all our brothers and sisters in the world, in whom we find your face!

We pray to you and glorify you for families, and especially those which give up to you a life from their home!

SEPTEMBER 9, 1990

Our Father who is in Heaven

Holy Father, friend of all creatures,
everlastingly in your Word
you loved us and thought of us
and wished us to recognize your face
in the face of your Only Begotten
born of Mary.
In him, tested in everything like us,
except sin,
you suffered our weaknesses;
in him your mercy extends
from generatin to generation forever.
Holy Father,
see your people
as, after celebrating the memory
of the Passion and death of the Lord,
they follow the Way of the Cross,
praying in expectation of the Resurrection.
We share your Son's cry of pain,
its echo continuing in the cry
that goes up from the countless crosses
of men and women of all epochs.
We are in communion
with his offering of love,
while his Passion draws to a close:
in the tragic period
of suffering and death
we pray that the trusting dialogue of us children
with you, Father,
in the Spirit of your Son
may never cease.
He lives and reigns forever and ever.

INITIAL PRAYER OF THE
VIA CRUCIS, APRIL 2, 1999

Prayer for the third year of preparation for the Great Jubilee of 2000

Blessed are you, Lord,
Father in Heaven,
because in your infinite mercy
you looked down on man's wretchedness
and gave us Jesus, your Son,
born of woman,
our Savior and friend,
brother and Redeemer.
Thank you, good Father,
for the gift of the Jubilee year;
let it be a favorable time,
the year of the great return to our Father's house,
where you, full of love,
await your lost children
to give them the embrace of forgiveness
and welcome them to your table,
clothed in holiday garments.

To you, Father, our eternal praise!

Most merciful Father,
in the Holy Year
may love for you flourish vigorously,
and for our neighbor, too:
may the disciples of Christ
promote justice and peace;
may the Good News
be proclaimed to the poor,
and let Mother Church direct
her preferential love
to the poor and the outcast.

To you, Father, our eternal praise!

Righteous Father,
may the great Jubilee be a propitious occasion
for all Catholics to rediscover the joy
of living attentive to your Word
and abandoned to your will;
may they feel the value
of fraternal communion,
breaking bread together
and praising you with hymns and spiritual songs.

To you, Father, our eternal praise!

O Father, rich in mercy,
may the Holy Jubilee be a time of openness,
of dialogue and meeting
among all the believers in Christ
and the followers of other religions.
In your immense love
be generous with mercy for all.

To you, Father, our eternal praise!

O God, Almighty Father,
let all your children know
that gentle Most Holy Mary accompanies
them on the road to you,
man's final destination:
she who is the icon of pure love,
chosen by you to be
the Mother of Christ and of the Church.

To you, Father, our eternal praise!

To you, Father of life,
the principle without principle,
the highest goodness and the eternal light,
with the Son and with the Spirit,
honor and glory, praise and gratitude,
to the end of time.
Amen.

Holy Friday

Christ Jesus! We are about to conclude this Holy Day of Holy Friday at the foot of your Cross. Just as long ago in Jerusalem your Mother, John, and Magdalene and other women stood at the foot of the Cross, so, too, we are here. We are profoundly moved by the importance of the moment. Words fail us in expressing all that our hearts feel. On this night—when, after taking you down from the Cross, they laid you in a tomb at the foot of Calvary—we wish to pray *that you will remain with us by way of your Cross:* you, who through the Cross separated yourself from us. We pray that you will remain with the Church; that you will remain with humanity; that you will not be dismayed if many, perhaps, pass by your Cross indifferently, if some keep their distance from it, and others do not get there.

And yet perhaps never more than today has man needed this power and this knowledge that you yourself are, you alone: by means of your Cross.

Then stay with us in this penetrating mystery of your death, in which you revealed how much "God loved the world." Stay with us and draw us to you, you who fell beneath this Cross. Stay with us through your Mother, to whom you, from the Cross, entrusted every man in particular.

Abide with us!

Stat Crux, dum volvitur orbis! Yes, "the Cross remains constant while the world turns!"

APRIL 11, 1979

79

"Lord, stay with us"

"Lord, stay with us."

The Disciples said these words for the first time in Emmaus. Later, in the course of centuries, they have been on the lips of so many of your disciples and confessors, innumerable times, O Christ.

I utter the same words, *to call on you,* Christ, in your Eucharistic presence, to welcome the daily worship lasting through the entire day, in this temple.

Stay with us today, and stay, from now on, every day.

Stay! So that we may *meet you* in the prayer of adoration and thanks, in the prayer of expiation and petition.

Stay! You who are at the same time *veiled* in the Eucharistic mystery of faith and *unveiled* under the species of bread and wine, which you have assumed in this Sacrament.

Stay! So that you may ceaselessly reconfirm your presence in this temple, and all those who enter may know that it is your house, "the dwelling of God among men," and find the very source of life and holiness that pours from your Eucharistic heart.

The Eucharist is the sacramental testimony of *your First Coming,* by which the words of the prophets have been confirmed and their expectations fulfilled. You left us, O Lord, your Body and your Blood under the species of bread and wine so that they might attest to the redemption of the world as it transpired — so that through them your Paschal Mystery might reach all men, as the Sacrament of Life and salvation. At the same time, the Eucharist is a steadfast herald of *your Second coming* and the sign of the ultimate Advent and the expectation of the whole Church: *"We announce your death, Lord, we proclaim your Resurrection, in expectation of your Coming."*

We long to worship you every day and every hour, stripped under the "species of bread and wine," to renew the hope of the *"call to glory"* whose beginning you established with your body glorified *"at the right hand of the Father."*

One day, O Lord, you asked Peter: *"Do you love me?"*

You asked him three times — and three times the Apostle answered: *"Lord, you know everything, you know that I love you."* Peter's answer is expressed *through* this adoration every day and all day.

All who participate in the adoration of your Eucharistic presence bear witness every time they do so, and make the truth contained in the words of the Apostle resound again: "Lord, you know everything; *you know that I love you.*"

Amen.

INAUGURATION OF THE PERMANENT
EXHIBITION OF THE EUCHARIST AT
ST. PETER'S, DECEMBER 2, 1981

Stay with us

Lord,
the day is already waning,
stay with us.
Stay to illuminate our doubts
and our fears.
Stay so that we may fortify
our light with yours.
Stay to help us be
strong and generous.
Stay so that in a world
that has little faith and hope
we may be able to encourage
one another
and sow faith and hope.
Stay
so that we, too, may learn from you
to be the light for other young people
and for the world.

APRIL 11, 1984

Eucharistic worship

Lord Jesus,
we are gathered here before you.
You are the Son of God made man,
crucified by us and raised up by the Father.
You, the living one,
actually present among us.
You, the way, the truth, and the life:
you, who alone have words of eternal life.
You, the sole foundation of our salvation
and the sole name to invoke
if we are to have hope.
You, the image of the Father
and the giver of the Spirit;
you, Love: Love not loved!
Lord Jesus, we believe in you,
we worship you,
we love you with all our heart,
and we proclaim your name above every other name.

In this solemn moment
we pray to you for our city.
Watch over it, O Christ, from your Cross,
and save it.
Watch over the poor, the sick,
the old people, the outcast,
the young men and girls
who have embarked on desperate roads,
the many families in trouble and afflicted by misfortune
and society's ills.
Look, and have pity!
Look at those who no longer know how to believe
in the Father who is in Heaven,

who no longer perceive his tenderness,
those who cannot
read in your face,
O Crucified One,
their pain, their poverty,
and their sufferings.
See how many are lying in sin,
far from you,
who are the source of living water:
the only one who takes away thirst
and soothes the yearning and restless anxiety
of the human heart.
Look at them and have pity!

Bless our city and our neighborhood.
Bless all the workers
who by their daily toil
see to the needs of families
and the progress of society.
Bless the young,
so that hope of a better world
is not extinguished in their hearts,
nor the wish to devote themselves generously
to build it.
Bless those who govern us,
that they may work for justice and peace.
Bless the priests
who lead the communities,
the men and women religious, the consecrated.
Bless the seminary and give to the diocese
generous young men and women
willing to accept the call
to give themselves completely to the service of the Gospel
and their brothers and sisters.

O Lord Jesus, allow
our parish community
to be confirmed
in the faith of baptism,
so that it may possess the joy of the truth,
the only road that leads to life!
Give it the grace of reconciliation
that spills from your pierced heart,
O Crucified One:
so that, reconciled and united,
it may become a force
that transcends divisions,
and, leavened by a new mentality
of solidarity and sharing,
is a living call to follow you
who became the brother of us all.
Finally, let it be a community that is a
messenger of hope for all men and women,
and may this testimony of hope
spur them to commit themselves,
to work for a
more united and peaceful world,
conforming to the will of your Father,
our Creator.

Lord Jesus
give us peace, you who are peace
and on your Cross transcended every division.
And make us
true workers for peace and justice:
men and women
who are committed to build
a world that is more just,
more united, and more fraternal.

Lord Jesus,
return among us
and make us vigilant
in expectation of your coming.
Amen.

JUNE 16, 1985

Prayer for families

Lord Jesus, we thank you because the Gospel of the Father's love, with which you came to save the world, has been proclaimed far and wide in America, as a gift of the Holy Spirit that fills us with gladness.

We thank you for the gift of your life, which you gave us by loving us to the end: it makes us children of God and brothers and sisters of each other. Increase our faith and our love for you, Lord, who are present in the many tabernacles of the continent.

Grant that we may be faithful witnesses to your Resurrection for the younger generations, so that knowing you they may follow you and find in you their peace and joy. Only then will they know that they are brothers and sisters of all God's children, scattered throughout the world. You, who, in becoming man, chose to belong to a human family, teach families the virtues that filled the house in Nazareth with light. May families always be united, as you and the Father are one, and be living witnesses to love, justice, and solidarity; make them schools of respect, forgiveness, and mutual help, so that the world may believe; help them to be a source of vocations to the priesthood, to the consecrated life, and all other forms of firm Christian commitment.

Protect your Church and the successor of Peter, to whom you, Good Shepherd, have entrusted the task of feeding your flock. Grant that your Church may flourish and grow richer in the fruits of holiness. Teach us to love your Mother, Mary, as you loved her. Give us the strength to proclaim your Word with courage in the work of the new evangelization, so that the world may know new hope.

ECCLESIA IN AMERICA
(APOSTOLIC EXHORTATION,
JANUARY 26, 1999)

Message for the World Day of Prayer for Vocations, 1998

Spirit of eternal love,
who proceeds from the Father and the Son,
we thank you for all the vocations
of Apostles and Saints
which have enriched the Church.
We beg you to continue
this work of yours.
Remember when, at Pentecost,
you descended on the Apostles
gathered together in prayer
with Mary, the Mother of Jesus,
and look at your Church today, which has
a particular need for holy priests,
for faithful and authoritative witnesses
of your grace;
she needs consecrated men and women,
who demonstrate the joy
of those who live only for the Father,
who make their own the mission
and the offering of Christ,
who build up in charity
the new world.
Holy Spirit,
eternal spring of joy and peace,
it is you who open heart and mind
to the divine call;
you who make effective
every impulse to the good,
to truth, to charity.

Your sighs too deep for words
rise up to the Father from the heart of the Church,
which suffers and struggles for the Gospel.
Open the hearts and minds
of young men and women,
so that a new flowering
of holy vocations
may show forth the fidelity of your love,
and all may know Christ,
the true light coming into the world
to offer to every human being
the sure hope of eternal life.
Amen.

Mother of Beautiful Love!

Hail, O Mother, Queen of the world.
You are the Mother of beautiful love,
you are the Mother of Jesus
the source of all grace,
the perfume of every virtue,
the mirror of all purity.
You are joy in distress,
victory in battle,
hope in death.
How sweet the taste
of your name on our lips,
how gentle the harmony
in our ears,
what ecstasy in our hearts!
You are happiness for those who suffer,
the crown of martyrs
the beauty of virgins.
We implore you that after this exile
you will lead us
to possess your Son, Jesus.
Amen.

Mary, star of evangelization

Mary, under the inspiration of the Holy Spirit, you said that the generations would call you blessed. We take up the hymn of past generations, so that it is not interrupted, and we exalt in you that which is most luminous, and which humanity offered to God: the human creature in its perfection, newly created in justice and holiness, in an incomparable beauty that we call "Immaculate" or "full of grace."

Mother, you are the "new Eve." The Church of your Son is aware that only with "new men" can there be evangelization, that is, can the Good News be brought to the world, so that, through your intercession, the newness of the Gospel — the seed of holiness and fruitfulness — is never absent from her.

Mary, we adore the Father for the qualities that shine in you, but we adore him also because for us you are always "the Handmaiden of the Lord," little creature. Because you were able to say, *"fiat"*—"let it be"—you became the Bride of the Holy Spirit and the Mother of the Son of God.

Mother, who appears in the pages of the Gospel showing Christ to the shepherds and the wise men, let every evangelizer — bishop, priest, religious, nun, father or mother, youth or child — be possessed by Christ so that he can reveal him to others.

Mary, who are hidden in the crowd while your Son performs the miraculous signs of the coming of the Kingdom of God, and who speak only to say that you will do all that he asks, help the evangelizers preach not themselves but Jesus Christ.

Mother, shrouded in the mystery of your Son, often without understanding, yet taking in everything and pondering in your heart, make us evangelizers aware that, beyond technology and strategy, preparations and plans, to evangelize is to immerse ourselves in the mystery of Christ and attempt to communicate something of him to our brothers and sisters.

Madonna of humility in truth, who taught us in the prophetic canticle that "God always exalts the humble," help "the simple and the poor," who seek you with popular piety, help the pastors guide them to the light of truth, and, when the pastors must eradicate elements that are no longer genuine and purify expressions of popular devotion, let them be strong and understanding at the same time.

Mother, like the Disciples at the Last Supper, we ask for your intercession, for the constant assistance of the Holy Spirit and the docility to welcome him in the Church; we ask for those who seek the truth of God and for those who must serve it and live it. May Christ forever be the "light of the world" and may the world recognize us as his disciples so that we may abide in his word and know the truth that will make us free with the freedom of children of God. So let it be.

JULY 8, 1980

Loving Comforter

O Most Holy Virgin, may you be the only and everlasting consolation of the Church whom you love and protect! Comfort your bishops and your priests, missionaries and religious, who must enlighten and save modern society, which is difficult and sometimes hostile. Comfort the Christian communities, by giving them the gift of many strong priestly and religious vocations!

Comfort all those who are charged with civil and religious, social and political authority and responsibility, so that they may have as their single, constant goal the common good and integral development of humanity, in spite of difficulties and defeats.

Comfort this people, which loves you and worships you; comfort the many immigrant families, the unemployed, the suffering, those who carry in body and soul the wounds caused by extreme situations; comfort the young, especially those who find themselves for so many painful reasons confused and discouraged; comfort those who feel in their hearts yearning for altruistic love, for charity, for self-giving, all those who cultivate high ideals of spiritual and social accomplishment.

O Mother and Comforter, comfort us all, and make all understand that the secret of happiness lies in goodness, and in faithfully following your son, Jesus.

APRIL 14, 1980

Act of Consecration to Mary, Fatima, May 13, 1982

"*We have recourse to your protection, Holy Mother of God!*"

Mother of individuals and peoples, you who "know all their sufferings and their hopes." You who have a mother's awareness of all the struggles between good and evil, between light and darkness, which afflict the modern world, hear our cry that, as if moved by the Holy Spirit, we address directly to your heart. Embrace, with the love of the Mother and the Handmaiden, this human world of ours, which we entrust and consecrate to you, for we are filled with concern for the earthly and eternal destiny of individuals and peoples.

In a special way we entrust and consecrate to you those individuals and *those nations* that particularly need to be entrusted and consecrated.

"*We have recourse to your protection, Holy Mother of God!*"

Do not reject the prayers that we who are in need send up to you!

Do not reject us!

Accept our humble trust — and our act of entrusting!

Before you, Mother of Christ, before your Immaculate heart, I today, together with the whole Church, unite myself with our Redeemer in this his consecration for the world and for people, which only in his divine heart has the power to obtain pardon and to secure reparation.

Above all may you be blessed, you, the Handmaiden of the Lord, who in the fullest way obey the divine call!

Hail to you, who *are wholly united* to the redeeming consecration of your Son!

Mother of the Church! Enlighten the people of God along the paths of faith, hope, and charity. Help us to live with the whole truth of the consecration of Christ, for the entire human family in the modern world.

In entrusting to you, O Mother, the world, all individuals and all peoples, *we also entrust to you the consecration itself,* for the world's sake, placing it in your motherly heart.

Oh, Immaculate Heart! Help us to vanquish the threat of evil, which so easily takes root in the hearts of the people of today, and whose immeasurable effects already weigh down on our modern world and seem to block the paths to the future!

From hunger and war, *deliver us!*

From nuclear war, from incalculable self-destruction, from every kind of war, *deliver us!*

From sins against the life of man from its very beginning, *deliver us!*

From hatred and from the demeaning of the dignity of the children of God, *deliver us!*

From every kind of injustice in the life of society, national, and international, *deliver us!*

From readiness to trample the commandments of God, *deliver us!*

From attempts to stifle in human hearts the very truth of God, *deliver us!*

From sins against the Holy Spirit, *deliver us! Deliver us!*

Accept, O Mother of Christ, this cry laden with the sufferings of all individuals, *laden with the sufferings* of whole societies!

May the infinite power of your *merciful love* be revealed yet again in the history of the world. May it stop evil! May it transform consciences! May your Immaculate Heart reveal for all the *light of hope!*

We consecrate ourselves to you

Hail Mary!
With the angel we greet you: full of grace.
The Lord is with you.
We greet you with Elizabeth. You are blessed among women,
and blessed is the fruit of your womb; blessed are you,
because you believed in the divine promises!
We greet you with the words of the Gospel:
You are blessed because you listened to the Word of God
and fulfilled it.

You are full of grace!
We praise you, beloved daughter of the Father.
We bless you, Mother of the divine Word.
We worship you, house of the Holy Spirit.
We call on you, Mother and model of the whole Church.
We contemplate you, the perfect image of the hopes of
all humanity.

The Lord is with you!
You are the Virgin of the Annunciation, the "yes" of all
humanity to the mystery of salvation.
You are the Daughter of Zion and the Ark of the
New Covenant in the mystery of the Visitation.
You are the Mother of Jesus who was born in Bethlehem,
she who showed him to the simple shepherds and to the
wise men of the east.
You are the Mother who presents her Son in the temple,
accompanies him into Egypt, leads him into Nazareth.
Virgin of the paths of Jesus, of the hidden life and of the
miracle at Cana.
Grieving Mother of Calvary and glorious Virgin of the
Resurrection.

You are the Mother of the Disciples of Jesus in the
    expectation and joy of Pentecost.

Blessed . . .
because you believed in the Word of the Lord
because you placed hope in his promises
because you were perfect in love
because of your attentive charity toward Elizabeth
for your maternal kindness in Bethlehem
for your strength in persecution,
for your perseverance in the search for Jesus in the temple,
for your simple life in Nazareth,
for your intercession in Cana,
for your maternal presence at the foot of the Cross,
for your faith in the expectation of Resurrection,
for your constant prayer at Pentecost.
You are blessed for the glory of your Assumption into Heaven
for your maternal protection of the Church
for your constant intercession for all mankind.

Holy Mary, Mother of God!
We wish to consecrate ourselves to you.
Because you are the Mother of God and our mother.
Because your Son Jesus entrusted us to you.
To you I consecrate the entire Church, with its pastors
    and its faithful.
The bishops, who in imitation of the Good Shepherd watch
    over the people who have been entrusted to them.
The priests, who have been anointed by the Spirit.
Men and women religious, who offer their lives to the
    Kingdom of Christ.
Seminarians, who have accepted the call of the Lord.
Christian husbands and wives, in the unity and
    indissolubility of their love and their families.
Lay people engaged in the Apostolate.

Young people who yearn for a new society.
Children, who deserve a more humane and peaceful world.
The sick, the poor, the incarcerated, the persecuted,
  orphans, the desperate, and those about to die.
To you I consecrate the entire nation, of which you are
  the Patroness and Queen.
May the values of the Gospel shine in its institutions.

Pray for us sinners!

Mother of the Church, we have recourse to your protection and we entrust ourselves to your inspiration.

We ask that the Church may be faithful in the purity of faith, in the steadfastness of hope, in the ardor of charity, in apostolic and missionary generosity, in the commitment to promote justice and peace among the children of this blessed earth.

We entreat you for the whole Church: that she may remain forever in the perfect communion of faith and love, united to the See of Peter by tight bonds of obedience and charity.

We pray to you for success in the new evangelization, for fidelity to preferential love for the poor and to the Christian formation of young people, for an increase in priestly and religious vocations, for generosity in those who devote themselves to the mission, to unity, and to the sanctity of families.

Now in the hour of our death!

Virgin in the Rosary, our Mother! Pray for us now.

Grant us the precious gift of peace.

Of forgiving all hatred and bitterness, and reconciling all our brothers and sisters.

May violence and warfare cease.

May dialogue progress and take root, and peaceful coexistence begin.

May new pathways of justice and prosperity be opened up. We ask this of you whom we invoke as the Queen of Peace. Now and in the hour of our death!

We entrust to you all the victims of injustice and violence, all those who have died in natural catastrophes, all those who in the hour of death turn to you as Mother and Patroness.

Be for all of us, Gate of Heaven, life, sweetness, and hope, so that together with you we may glorify the Father, the Son, and the Holy Spirit.

Amen!

JULY 3, 1986

Queen of Peace

Holy Virgin,
you who lived in faith
the difficult moments of family life,
secure peace for nations at war
and help the families of the world
to carry out their indispensable
mission of peace.

DECEMBER 12, 1993

Give us peace and unity

Holy Mother of God,
you who are vaster than Heaven,
since you contained in yourself
he whom Heaven cannot contain,
turn your maternal gaze toward this house
where men and women seek,
in the silence of listening
and in the communion of hearts,
a future of faith for Europe
where they strive to discover
what the hands of the men and women
of today, reaching out, wish to grasp.
Give them the peace of pilgrims
and the joy of walking together,
so that Europe, too,
may welcome more and more to its bosom,
as you welcomed
the Word of life,
the only hope of the world.

DECEMBER 12, 1993

Sustain us on the path of faith

Mother of the Redeemer,
joyfully we proclaim that you are blessed.
Before the world was created,
God the Father chose you
to fulfill his providential
plan of salvation.
You believed in his love
and obeyed his word.
The Son of God wanted you for his Mother,
when he became man to save man.
You received him
with eager obedience
and an undivided heart.
The Holy Spirit loved you
as his mystical spouse
and filled you with wonderful gifts.
Docilely you let yourself be molded
by his powerful hidden action.

On the eve of the third Christian millennium,
we entrust the Church to you,
she recognizes you and invokes you as her Mother.
You, who preceded her on earth
in the pilgrimage of faith,
comfort her in trials and tribulations,
and grant that she may be
an ever more effective
sign and instrument in the world
of the intimate union with God
and of the unity of the whole human race.

To you, Mother of individuals and nations,
we confidently entrust all humanity
with its hopes and fears.
Do not let the light
of true wisdom fail.
Guide us in the search for liberty
and justice for all.
Direct our steps along the paths of peace.
Let us all encounter Christ,
the way, the truth, and the life.
O Virgin Mary, sustain
us on the road of faith
and obtain for us the grace of eternal salvation.
O clement, O pious, O sweet Mother of God
and our Mother, Mary!

PRAYER FOR THE START OF
THE MARIAN YEAR,
JUNE 6, 1987

Mother of the risen Christ

O Mother of the Redeemer, who was crucified and is risen, Mother who became ours at the moment when Christ, by dying, performed the supreme act of his love for men, help us! Pray for us! We need to live, with you, as the risen. We must, and we will, let go of every demeaning compromise with sin; we must, and we will, walk with you, following Christ. *"Succurre cadenti surgere qui curat populo."* *(Assist your people who have fallen yet strive to rise again.)* Today we join the ancient Antiphon of Advent with the Antiphon of Easter: *"Resurrexit sicut dixit, alleluia! Ora pro nobis, Deum, alleluia."* *(He has risen as he said, alleluia. Pray for us, Lord, alleluia.)*

Your Son is risen; your Son prays for us. We, too, are risen with him; we, too, wish to live as the risen. Sustain us in this "unending challenge to human awareness . . . the challenge to follow, by both old means and new, the path of 'not falling,' which is the path of 'rising.' "

Ora pro nobis Deum! As we approach the third Christian millennium, pray for us, Lord! Deliver us from evil; from war, hatred, hypocrisy, mutual misunderstanding; from hedonism, impurity, selfishness, hardheartedness. Deliver us!

Ora pro nobis Deum! Alleluia.

APRIL 6, 1988

Watch over the Church, which is continuously threatened by the spirit of the world

Holy Mother of the Redeemer,
Gate of Heaven, Star of the Sea,
help your people, who yearn to rise.
Yet again
we turn to you,
Mother of Christ,
and of the Church.
We gather at your feet
to thank you
for what you have done
in these difficult years
for the Church,
for each of us,
and for all humanity.

"Show thyself a Mother":
how many times have we called on you!
And today we are here to thank you,
because you have always listened to us.
You showed that you are our Mother:
Mother of the Church,
missionary along the paths of the earth
in expectation of the third Christian millennium.
Mother of men,
for the constant protection
that has averted disasters
and irreparable destruction,
and has encouraged progress
and improvements in modern society.

Mother of nations
for the unhoped-for changes
that have given trust back to peoples
too long oppressed and humiliated.
Mother of life, for the many signs
with which you accompanied us,
defending us from evil
and from the power of death.
Mother of every man who struggles for the life
that does not die.
Mother of humanity
redeemed by the blood of Christ.
Mother of perfect love,
of hope and peace,
Holy Mother of the Redeemer.

"Show thyself a Mother":
Yes, continue to show that you are the Mother of us all,
because the world needs you.
The new situations
of peoples and the Church
are still precarious and unstable.
The danger exists
of replacing Marxism
with another form of atheism,
which, idolizing freedom,
tends to destroy
the roots of human and Christian morality.
Mother of hope, walk with us!
Walk with mankind
at the very end
of the twentieth century,
with men of every race and culture,
of every age and state.

Walk with peoples
toward solidarity and love,
walk with the young,
the protagonists of future days of peace.
The nations that have recently
regained their freedom
and are now engaged
in constructing their future
have need of you.
Europe needs you,
which from east to west
cannot find
its identity
without rediscovering
its common Christian roots.
The world needs you
to resolve
the many violent
conflicts that still
threaten it.

"Show thyself a Mother":
Show that you are the Mother of the poor,
of those who are dying of hunger and sickness,
of those who suffer injustice and tyranny,
of those who cannot find work, home, or refuge,
of those who are oppressed and exploited,
of those who despair or in vain seek
tranquillity far from God.
Help us to defend life,
the reflection of divine love,
help us to defend it forever,
from dawn to its natural sunset.
Show yourself the Mother of unity and peace.

May violence and injustice cease everywhere,
may harmony and unity
grow within families,
and respect and understanding among peoples;
may peace, true peace, reign upon the earth!
Mary, give Christ, our peace, to the world.
Do not let peoples reopen new abysses
of hatred and vengeance,
do not let the world yield to the seductions
of a false well-being
that perverts the value of the human person
and forever compromises
the natural resources of Creation.
Show yourself the Mother of hope!
Watch over the road that still awaits us.
Watch over men
and over the new situations of peoples
still threatened by the risk of war.
Watch over those responsible for nations
and those who rule the destiny of humanity.
Watch over the Church,
which is constantly threatened by the spirit of the world.

In collegial unity with the pastors, and
in communion with the entire people of God,
who are scattered to the far corners of the earth,
I today renew humanity's
filial trust in you.
To you we all with confidence entrust ourselves.
With you we hope to follow Christ,
the Redeemer of man: may our weariness
not weigh on us, nor our toil slacken us;
let not obstacles quench our courage,
nor sadness the joy in our hearts.

You, Mary, Mother of the Redeemer,
continue to show that you are the Mother of all,
watch over our path,
so that, full of joy, we may see
your Son in Heaven.
Amen.

ACT OF ENTRUSTMENT TO THE
VIRGIN OF FATIMA, MAY 13, 1991

Message for the World Day of
Prayer for Vocations, 1995

O Virgin of Nazareth,
the "yes" spoken in youth
marked your existence
and it grew as did your life itself.
O Mother of Jesus,
in your free and joyous "yes"
and in your active faith
so many generations and so many teachers
have found inspiration and strength
for welcoming the Word of God
and for doing his will.
O Teacher of life,
teach young people
to pronounce the "yes"
that gives meaning to existence
and lets them discover the hidden "name" of God
in the heart of each of us.
O Queen of the Apostles,
give us wise teachers,
who will know how to love young people and help them grow,
guiding them to the encounter with Truth
that makes us free and happy.
Amen!

Help us respect Creation

O Mary,
radiant with singular beauty,
help us appreciate and respect Creation.
You who are so beloved
by the people of the mountains,
and in these valleys
are worshiped in so many sanctuaries,
protect the valleys' inhabitants,
so that they may be faithful to their traditions
and at the same time open and hospitable.
Help us to make our lives
an ascension toward God
and to follow forever Jesus Christ, your Son,
who guides us to our goal,
where, in the new Creation,
we will enjoy the fullness of life and peace.

JULY 11, 1999

For the unity of all Christians

Let us pray for the unity of all Christians! This great gift that only God can grant can transform hearts, divisions, and the wounds of centuries, and expand the prayer that Jesus addressed to the Father for the unity of his Disciples: "That they may all be one; even as thou art in me, and I in thee." With this prayer we begin the ecumenical week, turning to our Christian brothers who are not yet fully united with us, and we invoke this unity as a gift from on high.

Amen!

January 19, 1992

Evangelize, reflect, pray

Let us pray
together with the Most Holy Virgin, trusting in her intercession.
Let us pray
that the holy mysteries of the Rising and of the Holy Spirit may enlighten many generous people, ready and willing to serve the Church.
Let us pray
for the pastors and for their helpers, so that they may find the right words in which to bring the faithful the message of the priestly and consecrated life.
Let us pray
that in all areas of the Church the faithful may believe with renewed fervor in the evangelical ideal of the priest who is completely devoted to building up the Kingdom of God, and that they may encourage such vocations with decisive generosity.
Let us pray
for young people, to whom the Lord addresses the call to follow him more nearly, so that they may not be led astray by the things of this world but will open their hearts to the friendly voice that calls them; so that they may be able to devote themselves for their whole life, "with an undivided heart," to Christ, to the Church, to other souls; so that they may believe that grace bestows on them strength for such giving, and that they may see the beauty and grandeur of the priestly, religious, and missionary life.
Let us pray
for families, that they may succeed in creating a Christian climate that fosters the important religious choices of their children. At the same time, we thank the Lord from the bottom of our hearts, because in recent years, in many parts of the world, young people, and others, are responding in increasing numbers to the divine call.

Let us pray

that all priests and religious may be to those who are called an example and an inspiration by their availability and their humble eagerness "to accept the gifts of the Holy Spirit and to bestow on others the fruits of love and peace, to give them that certainty of faith from which derives a profound comprehension of the sense of human life and the capacity to introduce a moral order into the lives of individuals and their environments."

1980

Young people, Christ calls you

God our Father,
we entrust to you the young men
and young women of the world,
with their problems,
aspirations, and hopes.
Keep your loving gaze on them
and make them workers of peace
and builders of the civilization of love.
Call them to follow Jesus, your Son.
Help them to understand the value
of giving their lives fully
for you and for humanity.
Let their response be
generous and eager.
Accept also, Lord,
our praise and our prayer
for the young people who,
following the example of Mary, the Mother of the Church,
believed in your word
and are preparing for Holy Orders,
for the profession of the evangelical counsels,
for the missionary commitment.
Help them to understand that the call
you have given them
is always present and urgent.
Amen.

1985

Consider the call

Lord Jesus,

Just as you called the first Disciples to make them fishers of men, so may you continue to make your sweet call heard today: "Come, follow me!"

Give young men and women the grace to respond readily to your voice.

Sustain our bishops, priests, and consecrated people in their Apostolic labors. Let our seminarians persevere, along with all who are achieving the ideal of a life totally devoted to your service.

Reawaken in our communities the missionary commitment. Lord, send laborers into your harvest and do not let mankind go astray because there are not enough pastors, missionaries, and others vowed to the cause of the Gospel.

Mary, Mother of the Church,

model for every vocation, help us to answer "yes" to the Lord who calls us to collaborate in the divine plan of salvation.

1987

Mother of priests

O Mary,
Mother of Jesus Christ and Mother of priests,
accept this title which we bestow on you
to celebrate your motherhood
and to contemplate with you the priesthood
of your Son and of your sons,
O Holy Mother of God.

O Mother of Christ,
to the Messiah-priest you gave a body of flesh
through the anointing of the Holy Spirit
for the salvation of the poor and the contrite of heart;
guard priests in your heart and in the Church,
O Mother of the Savior.

O Mother of Faith,
you accompanied to the Temple the Son of Man,
the fulfillment of the promises given to the fathers;
give to the Father for his glory
the priests of your Son,
O Ark of the Covenant.

O Mother of the Church,
in the midst of the Disciples in the upper room
you prayed to the Spirit
for the new people and their shepherds;
obtain for the Order of Presbyters
a full measure of gifts,
O Queen of the Apostles.

O Mother of Jesus Christ,
you were with him at the beginning
of his life and mission,
you sought the Master among the crowd,
you stood beside him when he was lifted
up from the earth
consumed as the one Eternal Sacrifice,
and you had John, your son, near at hand;
accept from the beginning those
who have been called,
protect their growth,
in their life ministry accompany
your sons,
O Mother of priests.
Amen.

PASTORES DABO VOBIS
(APOSTOLIC EXHORTATION, MARCH 25, 1992)

Pastores dabo vobis

Pastores dabo vobis: with these words the whole Church addresses you, who are the Lord of the harvest, asking for laborers for your harvest, which is plentiful. Good Shepherd, long ago you sent the first workers into your harvest. They were twelve. Now that almost two millenniums have passed, and their voice has traveled to the ends of the earth, we, too, feel profoundly the need to pray that there will be no shortage of successors to them for our time — and, in particular, no shortage of men in the ministerial priesthood, who build up the Church with the power of the Word of God and the Sacraments; who in your name administer the Eucharist, from which the Church continually grows, the Church which is your Body.

We thank you, because the temporary crisis of vocations, in the context of the universal Church, is on the way to being resolved. With great joy we have seen a strong renewal of vocations in various parts of the globe: in the young churches, but also in the many nations of a centuries-old Christian tradition, not to mention places where, in our century, the Church has been harshly persecuted. But we raise our prayer with special fervor as we think of those societies in which the climate of secularization dominates, in which the spirit of this world inhibits the action of the Holy Spirit, so that the seed scattered in the souls of the young either does not take root or does not mature. For those societies, in particular, we implore you even more eagerly: *"Send forth your Spirit and renew the face of the earth."*

The Church thanks you, O divine Bridegroom, because from the earliest times she accepted the call to consecrated celibacy for the sake of the Kingdom of God; because for centuries she has preserved the charism of the celibacy of priests. We thank you for the Second Vatican Council and for the recent Synods of bishops, which, affirming this charism, pointed to it as a just path for the

Church of the future. We are aware how fragile are the vessels in which we carry this treasure—yet we believe in the power of the Holy Spirit who works through the grace of the Sacrament in each of us. Even more fervently we ask that we may be able to collaborate with this power and persevere.

We ask you, who are the Spirit of Christ the Good Shepherd, to remain faithful to this particular inheritance of the Latin Church. *"Do not quench the Spirit,"* the Apostle tells us. We therefore ask not to fall into doubt or sow doubts in others, not to become— God preserve us!—supporters of different choices and of a different spirituality for life and the mystery of the priesthood. St. Paul says again: *"And do not grieve the Holy Spirit of God . . ."*

Pastores dabo vobis!

We pray to you to forgive all our sins before the Holy Mystery of your priesthood in our life. We ask that we may be able to collaborate and persevere in this "plentiful harvest," and do all that is necessary to inspire and nurture vocations. Above all, we ask you to help us pray with constancy. You yourself said: *"Pray therefore the Lord of the harvest to send out laborers into his harvest."*

As we confront this world, which in various ways displays indifference toward the Kingdom of Heaven, may we be accompanied by the certainty that you, Good Shepherd, instilled in the hearts of the Apostles: *"Be of good cheer; I have overcome the world!"* This is—in spite of everything—the same world that your Father loved so much that he gave it to you, his Only Begotten Son.

Mother of the Divine Son, Mother of the Church, Mother of all peoples—pray with us! Pray for us!

NOVEMBER 30, 1992

Message for the World Day of Prayer for Vocations, 1999

Good Father,
in Christ your Son you reveal to us your love,
you embrace us as your children,
and you offer us the possibility of discovering
in your will the features
of our true face.
Holy Father,
you call us to be holy
as you are holy.
We pray that you may never allow your Church
to lack holy priests and Apostles
who, with the Word and the Sacraments,
will open the way to the encounter with you.
Merciful Father, give
to lost humanity men and women who,
through the witness of a life transfigured
to the image of your Son,
may walk joyously with
their other brothers and sisters
toward our heavenly homeland.
Our Father,
with the voice of your Holy Spirit,
and trusting in the maternal
intercession of Mary,
we earnestly beseech you:
send to your Church priests,
who will be courageous witnesses
of your infinite bounty.
Amen!

Brotherhood, peace, and love

Let us pray that the world may never again see a day as terrible as that when the bomb was dropped on Hiroshima.

Let us pray that men will never again place their trust, their calculation, their prestige in weapons so unspeakable and so immoral.

Let us pray that all nations will join together and agree to ban the deadly capacity to construct, multiply, and maintain such weapons, which are the terror of all peoples.

Let us pray that that lethal explosion did not, in seeking peace, also kill it; did not wound forever the honor of science; and did not extinguish the serenity of life on earth.

Let us pray that brotherhood, peace, and love may be granted instead and assured to the world. Let us remember that only Christ can guarantee us the supreme gifts: only he, our Savior, who became our Brother, when Mary said, "Let it be," and became the Mother of Christ.

AUGUST 4, 1985

O Lord, help us build a culture without violence

O Lord and God of everything, you willed that all your children, united by the Spirit, should live and grow together in mutual acceptance, in harmony and peace. Our hearts are overflowing with affliction, because our human selfishness and greed have kept your plan from being accomplished in our time.

We recognize that peace is a gift that comes from you. We know, too, that our collaboration as your instruments requires that we manage the resources of the earth wisely, for the true progress of all peoples. It requires a profound respect and veneration for life, a lively regard for human dignity and the sacredness of each person's conscience, and a constant struggle against all forms of discrimination, in law and deed.

Together with all our brothers and sisters, we undertake to develop a deeper awareness of your presence and your action in history, to be more effective in truth and responsibility, and to work untiringly for freedom from all forms of oppression, brotherhood across every barrier, and justice and fullness of life for all.

We invoke your blessing on the leaders of this nation and all nations, on the followers of all religious traditions, and on all men of good will. Enable us, O Lord, to live and grow in active cooperation with you and all others, with the common aim of building a culture without violence, a world community that entrusts its security not to the construction of deadly weapons but to mutual trust and eagerness to work for a better future for all your children, in a *world civilization built of love, truth, and peace.*

FEBRUARY 2, 1986

Workers for peace

We wish to be workers for peace, because we recognize in creation the signs of God's wisdom, and we wish to live in peace, welcoming the gift of creation as a "good thing," as a sign and Sacrament of God's eternal love for all who live on this planet.

We place our hopes in the heart of Mary, the Mother of the Redeemer, relying on her loving care. To her, the Mother of God and our mother, we entrust the contemporary world's expectations of peace, the expectations of a time so full of significant events, so rich in profound changes. To her we entrust our intense desire that justice and love may prevail over all temptations to violence, revenge, corruption. We ask her that the word of the Gospel, the voice of Christ the Redeemer, may reach the hearts of all people through the mission of the Church.

In this period of the life of mankind, when we feel, with increasing evidence, how important are the obligations and the values of solidarity among nations, of consciously working toward an authentic world community, and are aware, too, of the cost, we ask God to help us respond to the gift of reconciliation, and build the hoped-for civilization of love.

We entrust our prayer to the Mother of the Redeemer, who was born in Bethlehem, so that God may turn his face toward us and grant us peace.

JANUARY 1, 1990

No more war!

God of our Fathers,
great and merciful,
Lord of peace and of life,
Father of all.

Your plan is for peace and not for suffering,
you condemn war
and you humble the pride of the aggressor.

You sent your son Jesus
to proclaim peace near and far,
to unite men
of every race and every ethnicity
in a single family.

Hear the unanimous cry of your children,
the heartfelt supplication of all humanity:
no more war, an adventure without return,
no more war,
a spiral of grief and violence.

In communion with Mary, the Mother of Jesus,
we pray to you again:
speak to the hearts of those who decide
the destinies of peoples,
stop the cycle of retaliation
and revenge,
suggest with your Spirit new solutions,
generous and honorable gestures,
periods of dialogue and patient waiting

more fruitful than the swift actions
of war.

Grant in our time days of peace.
No more war.
Amen.

JANUARY 16, 1991

Let us pray for peace

Brothers and sisters,

Anxiety and distress, which, unfortunately, have been expressed many times already over the war going on in the Gulf region, continue to be nourished by the persistent conflicts, and now, in addition, there are also catastrophic environmental risks.

The victims, both civilian and military, and the enormous destruction intensify our grief, and we are all called upon to address the Lord more insistently and with a stronger faith: it is the great recourse available to those who believe and have hope in divine mercy.

Let us pray above all for peace: that God may grant it as soon as possible, enlightening our leaders so that they may quickly abandon that road which is unworthy of humanity, and seek justice confidently through dialogue and negotiation! May the efforts of those who, generously, continue to propose initiatives to stop the conflict be crowned with success.

Let us pray for the civilian populations that are enduring bombardments or have been forced, in the hundreds of thousands, to abandon their homes and their native land, and to face the tragic experience of refugees: may God grant them comfort and inspire in all people feelings and initiatives of real solidarity!

Let us pray that the tragedy that is taking place does not become more brutal and inhuman through actions unacceptable in terms of both ethical values and international treaties. The news that has reached us concerning the fate of prisoners of war and the threat of recourse to the weapons of terrorism is a particular cause of anguish.

May God remove the temptation to use such means, which are contrary to the most elementary moral principles and condemned by international law!

Let us pray again for and with all believers belonging to the three religions that have their historical roots in the Middle East: Jews,

Christians, and Muslims. Faith in the same God must be a cause not of conflict and rivalry but of a commitment to overcome differences through dialogue and negotiations.

May the infinite love of the Creator help all to understand the absurdity of a war in his name and instill in every heart true feelings of trust, understanding, and cooperation for the good of all humanity!

We faithfully entrust these aims to the Most Holy Virgin, Queen of Peace.

JANUARY 27, 1991

May the peace given by your Son flourish

God of our Fathers,
Father of all,
who in your Son Jesus, the Prince of Peace,
proclaimed peace near and far,
to unite men
of every race and every creed
in a single family,
we implore you to grant
life without end and your peace
to the dead on all fronts,
who, many unidentified, lie
in this earth, which is bathed in their blood.
May their sacrifice and their heroism —
while opening hearts to gratitude
and reviving the great ideals of freedom
and love on mother earth —
arouse the desire for tolerance,
nonviolence, and peace.
For this reason, in communion with Mary,
the Mother of Jesus,
we pray, O Father,
that all those who climb
the steps of this memorial chapel
may be enlightened by the Spirit of your Son
and develop in their hearts
the desire to work for peace,
for all creatures.
Enlighten the leaders of nations,
so that, in view of the lesson
that history demonstrates,
they will no longer entrust to war the job

of resolving the problems
of living together among peoples.
May the peace given by your Son,
crucified and risen,
flourish in our lands,
and bring to men and women
in our time
a taste for developing those values
which build up your Kingdom
and never fade.
Amen.

MAY 3, 1992

Prayer for the Synod on the family

God, who are the Father of everything in Heaven and on earth, Father, who are love and life, make every human family on the earth become, through your Son Jesus Christ, "born of woman," and through the Holy Spirit, the source of divine charity, a true sanctuary of life and love for the generations to come. May your grace direct the thoughts and deeds of spouses to the good of their families and all the families of the world. May the younger generations find in the family strong support for their humanity, so that they may grow in truth and love. May love, strengthened by the grace of the Sacrament of Matrimony, prove to be stronger than any weakness or crisis that, at any time, our families must endure. Finally we ask you that the Church, through the intercession of the Holy Family of Nazareth, may successfully complete among all the nations of the earth her mission in the family through the family. You, who are life, the truth, and love, in the unity of the Son and the Holy Spirit. Amen.

AUGUST 15, 1980

Confidence in families

May St. Joseph, "the just man," a tireless worker, the upright guardian of those entrusted to his care, guard, protect, and enlighten families forever.

May the Virgin Mary, who is the Mother of the Church, thus also be the Mother of the "Church of the home." Thanks to her motherly aid, may every Christian family truly become a "little church," in which the mystery of the Church of Christ is mirrored and given new life. May she, the Handmaiden of the Lord, be an example of humble and generous acceptance of the will of God; may she, the sorrowful Mother at the foot of the Cross, comfort the sufferings and dry the tears of those who are in distress because of the difficulties in their families.

And may Christ the Lord, the Universal King, the King of families, be present in every Christian home as he was at Cana, bestowing light, joy, serenity, and strength. On the solemn day dedicated to his Kingship I beg of him that every family may generously make its own contribution to the coming of his Kingdom in the world—"a Kingdom of Truth and Life, a Kingdom of Holiness and Grace, a Kingdom of justice, love, and peace," toward which history is journeying.

I entrust each family to him, to Mary, to Joseph. To their hands and their hearts I offer this Exhortation: may it be they who present it to you, venerable brothers and beloved sons and daughters, and who open your hearts to the light that the Gospel sheds on every family.

FAMILIARIS CONSORTIO

In prayer for the family

We offer special thanks at this time for the Christian families of our parish.

Together with his son Jesus Christ our Lord, we thank the Father "from whom every family takes its name."

We thank him:

— For all the many families of the parish whose life reflects "the beauty and grandeur of the vocation to love and the service of life";

Lord, bless our families.

— For the deep love that Christian spouses exchange in the communion of marital life, keeping alive in the world an utterly special image of the love of God;

Lord, bless our families.

— For the life of mutual faith lived by innumerable couples, thanks to the power of Sacramental Grace;

Lord, bless our families.

— For all those couples who strive generously to follow God's plan of human love, which is expressed by the teaching of the Church in *Humanae Vitae* and *Familiaris Consortio,* and whose marriage is always open to new life; and for all those who help educate couples in natural family planning;

Lord, bless our families.

— For the great, extraordinary service rendered by parents in bringing new members to the mystical body of Christ;

Lord, bless our families.

— For the continuing involvement of fathers and mothers in the education of their children to Christian maturity;

Lord, bless our families.

— For families who despite suffering, pain, and economic hardship live a life of Christian hope;

Lord, bless our families.

—For the commitment of families, in conformity with the teaching of the Second Vatican Council, to participate actively in the mission of the Church, as a community of believers and evangelizers and as a community in dialogue with God and in the service of man;

Lord, bless our families.

—For the efforts of Christian families to help young people understand the dignity of marriage and prepare themselves adequately for this vocation;

Lord, bless our families.

—For the renewed commitment of the Church to support and teach the holiness and the unity of the family, and for the generous love with which so many priests and religious dedicate their energies to building family life;

Lord, bless our families.

—For the efforts of those families that have encountered problems and difficulties but have persevered in the conviction that the eternal and indestructible love of God for man is expressed in the indissoluble bond of their sacramental marriage;

Lord, bless our families.

—For the special testimony to Christ's teaching on the indissolubility of marriage given by all spouses who suffer the pain of separation, abandonment, or rejection;

Lord, bless our families.

—For spreading the message of the Gospel among Christian families, and for the evangelization that is carried out by families among their neighbors and in their workplace;

Lord, bless our families.

—For the many families that pray together and draw strength from the worship of God;

Lord, bless our families.

—For the families that embrace the Cross and share in the Christian joy of the Paschal Mystery of the Lord Jesus;

Lord, bless our families.
We give thanks to you and praise you,
God our Father,
for all the Christian families
who listen to the words of life
of Jesus Christ your Son:
"Let your light so shine
before men,
that they may see your good works
and give glory to your Father
who is in Heaven."
May we, together with all the families
of our parish,
respond to the Christian vocation,
each of us according to the gifts we have received,
each through the witness
of our good works
May each of us
hear the call
to give glory to you,
Lord our God,
Through Christ our Lord.
Amen.

SEPTEMBER 12, 1984

Prayer to the Holy Family

O Holy Family of Nazareth,
the community of love
of Jesus, Mary, and Joseph,
the model and ideal of every Christian family,
to you we entrust our families.

Open the heart of every home
to faith, to acceptance of the Word of God
to Christian witness,
so that it may become the source
of new and holy vocations.

Prepare the minds of parents,
so that, with urgent charity,
wise care, and loving piety,
they may guide their children surely
in the direction of spiritual and eternal goods.

Inspire in the souls of the young
an upright conscience and a free will,
so that, growing in "wisdom,
age, and grace,"
they may generously accept
the gift of the divine vocation.

O Holy Family of Nazareth,
make us all available to carry out the will of God,
by contemplating and imitating
the assiduous prayer,
the generous obedience,
the dignified poverty,

and the virginal purity lived in you,
and to accompany with prudent delicacy
those among us who are called
to follow more nearly the Lord Jesus,
who "gave himself" for us.
Amen.

1994

O Holy Family

be a guide for families everywhere on earth!

Family, Holy Family, may your example guide us and protect us!

Family, Holy Family— the Family so closely united to the mystery that we contemplate on the day of the Lord's birth, may your example guide families everywhere on earth!

Son of God, who came among us in the warmth of a family, grant that all families may grow in love and contribute to the good of mankind through a commitment to faithful and fruitful unity, respect for life, and a striving for brotherly solidarity with all.

Teach them, therefore, to put aside selfishness, lying, and unrestrained greed.

Help them to develop the immense resources of their hearts and minds, which multiply when it is you who inspire them.

Baby Jesus, dry
the tears of children!

Caress the old and the sick!

Urge men to lay down their weapons and hold each other in a universal embrace.

Invite all peoples, merciful Jesus, to tear down the walls created by misery and by unemployment, by ignorance and indifference, by discrimination and intolerance.

It is you, divine Child of Bethlehem, who save us, delivering us from sin.

It is you who are the true and only Savior, toward whom humanity gropes its way.

God of peace, gift of peace for all humanity, come and dwell in the heart of every man and every family.

Be our peace and our joy!

DECEMBER 25, 1994

Hasten, people

Christians of every continent,
committed to the difficult but necessary
road of unity and peace, and you, men of good will
who listen to me,
let us hasten, pilgrims all,
to the manger of Bethlehem.
Into the stable, where Jesus
speaks of innocence and peace,
we enter to listen to
a fundamental lesson.
Hasten, O humanity, scattered and fearful,
to beg for peace, a gift and task
for every individual of noble and generous feeling.
Enough of hatred and tyranny!
No more war.
No more indifference and silence
toward those who ask for understanding and solidarity,
toward the laments of those who are
dying of hunger,
among the waste and abundance of goods.
How can we forget those who suffer,
who are alone or abandoned, depressed and discouraged,
who have neither home nor job,
who are victims of oppression and abuse,
and of the many forms of
modern totalitarianism?
How can we allow economic interests
to reduce the human person
to an instrument of profit,
allow creatures not yet born
to be killed,

innocent children
to be humiliated and taken advantage of,
the old and the sick
to be outcast and abandoned?
Only you, Word Incarnate, born of Mary,
can make us brothers and sisters,
children in the Child,
children in the semblance of the Child.
Future glory was revealed to us
through you, the Son of Mary,
the Son of Man,
whence we can cry out: "Abba, Father!"
through you . . .
Amen!

DECEMBER 25, 1991

Young people, believe and you will live!

Because you exist, there is someone who has reserved something great for you. Listen to me, for I am about to announce it! Just as the Apostles Peter and John said to the man who, dressed in rags and lame from birth, was begging at the entrance to the Temple in Jerusalem, the Pope says to you: *"I have no silver or gold, but I give you what I have: in the name of Jesus Christ of Nazareth, walk!"* Yes, young friends, the Pope has come here today to *give you the strength of Christ, to give you a companion you may have confidence in!*

Can you have confidence, even just once, in someone who has never disappointed anyone? Open your heart to Jesus Christ and you will know the courage that never fails, however great the obstacles: you will know a love stronger than death! In the presence of this multitude of young people, I cannot help bearing witness to this power of God, praising this sure love that has already saved my life from death!

Young people, believe and you will live!

Young people, believe

and bet everything on love!

Young people,

believe and decide this very day

to build in your life a structure for eternity! My young friends and brothers, find again the faith in yourselves and build your lives, your love, your families in Christ! Because: *"I am sure that neither death, nor life, nor angels, nor pincipalities, nor things present, nor things to come, nor powers, nor height, nor depth, nor anything else in all creation, will be able to separate us from the love of God in Christ Jesus our Lord."* A young person faithful to Christ will know true happiness that has no end.

JUNE 7, 1992

Man of our time!

Man, you who live immersed in the world,
believing that you are its master
when perhaps you are its prey,
Christ will free you from every bond
to launch you in the conquest of yourself,
in constructive love, extended to the good;
exacting love,
that makes you the builder, not the destroyer,
of your tomorrow, of your family,
of your environment, of the whole society.
Man of our time!
Only Christ Resurrected
can satisfy fully
your unsuppressible aspiration to freedom.
After the atrocities of two world wars
and all the wars that,
in these fifty years,
often in the name of atheist ideologies,
have mowed down victims
and sowed hatred in so many nations;
after years of dictatorships
that have deprived man
of his fundamental freedoms,
the true dimensions of the spirit
have been rediscovered,
those which the Church has always promoted,
revealing in Christ the true stature of man.
Also, the awakening of many democracies
leads today to dialogue
and trust among peoples;
and the world understands again

that man cannot live without God!
Without the Truth that, in him, makes man free.
Man of our time!
Christ frees you from selfishness
and calls you to share,
and to a swift and joyous
commitment to others.
Man of today!
Wealthy nations of an opulent civilization!
Do not be indifferent to the world's many tragedies,
be increasingly aware of the need
to help those peoples
who struggle every day
for survival.
Believe that there is no freedom
where misery persists.
May human and Christian solidarity be
the challenge that stimulates your conscience
so that the sand
may yield a little at a time
to the promotion of human dignity,
and make the bread take shape
to give back a smile, work,
hope, progress.
But, thanks to God, I have also seen
single people, associations, institutions,
priests, religious, lay people in various professions
voluntarily commit themselves and sacrifice themselves
for the good of their lonely and suffering brothers and sisters.
I thank them in the name of Christ crucified and risen!
Man of our time!
Christ *frees you because he loves you,*
because he gave himself for you
because he overcame for you and for all men.

Christ restored the world and you to God.
He restored God to you and to the world.
Forever!
"Be of good cheer, I have overcome the world!"
With this complete confidence
in Christ's love
for man who lives, hopes, suffers,
and loves in every latitude
of the globe,
I greet the various peoples and nations,
in their own languages,
and wish for all of you the joy and
the peace of the Risen Christ.

APRIL 15, 1990

From
The Rosary Hour

The Rosary, the summary of the whole Gospel

As you know, tomorrow is the start of the month of October, which Christian piety has linked, in particular, to a more committed and devout daily recitation of the Holy Rosary, which my predecessors Pius XII and Paul VI called *"the summary of the whole Gospel."* For centuries this prayer has held an honored place in the worship of the Blessed Virgin, *"under whose protection the faithful, praying, take refuge in all dangers and times of need."*

The Rosary is a simple prayer but at the same time theologically rich in Biblical references; for this reason Christians love it and recite it frequently and fervently, well aware of its authentic "Gospel nature," which Paul VI speaks of in the Apostolic Exhortation on the worship of the Blessed Virgin.

In the Rosary we meditate on the principal events of salvation that were accomplished in Christ: from the virgin conception to the final moments of the Passion and the glorification of the Mother of God. This is a prayer of continuous praise and supplication to Most Holy Mary, that she may intercede for us, poor sinners, in every moment of our day, until the hour of our death.

So I wish to urge you, in the month of October, to rediscover the Holy Rosary and to value it more highly as a personal and family prayer, addressed to she who is the Mother of faithful individuals and the Mother of the Church.

SEPTEMBER 30, 1981

The simplicity and the profundity of the Rosary

Now, at the end of October, I would like, along with you, my brothers and sisters, to examine the simultaneous simplicity and profundity of this prayer, to which the Most Holy Mother invites us, urges us, and encourages us. In reciting the Rosary, we penetrate the Mysteries of the life of Jesus, which are at the same time the Mysteries of his Mother.

This can be seen clearly in the Joyful Mysteries, beginning with the Annunciation, through the Visitation and the birth on that night in Bethlehem, and later in the presentation of the Lord, until he is found in the temple, when he was already twelve years old.

Although it may seem that the Sorrowful Mysteries do not directly show us the Mother of Jesus — with the exception of the last two: the Via Crucis and the Crucifixion — how could we even imagine that the Mother was spiritually absent when her Son was suffering so terribly in Gethsemane, during his scourging and crowning with thorns?

And the Glorious Mysteries are in fact Mysteries of Christ, in which we find the *spiritual presence* of Mary — and first of all is the Mystery of the Resurrection. The Holy Scripture does not mention the presence of Mary when it describes the Ascension — but must she not be present, if immediately afterward we read that she was in the Upper Room with the Apostles themselves, who had just said farewell to Christ as he rose to Heaven? Together with them, Mary prepared for the coming of the Holy Spirit and shared in the Pentecost of his descent. The last two Glorious Mysteries direct our thoughts toward the Mother of God, when we contemplate her Assumption and coronation in celestial glory.

The Rosary is a prayer *about Mary* united with Christ in his mission as the Savior. At the same time it is a prayer *to Mary* — our best mediator with her Son. It is, finally, a prayer that in a special way we say *with Mary,* just as the Apostles at the Last Supper prayed with her, preparing to receive the Holy Spirit.

OCTOBER 28, 1981

Mary prays for us and with us

"She was greatly troubled at the saying, and considered in her mind what sort of greeting this might be . . ."

The evangelist Luke says that Mary "was greatly troubled" at the words of the Angel Gabriel, addressed to her at the moment of the Annunciation, and *"considered in her mind what sort of greeting this might be."*

This meditation of Mary's constitutes the first model for the prayer of the Rosary. It is the prayer of those who hold dear the angel's greeting to Mary. People who recite the Rosary take up Mary's meditation in their thoughts and their hearts, and as they recite they ponder *"what sort of greeting this might be."*

First of all they repeat the words addressed to Mary by God himself, through his messenger.

Those who hold dear the angel's greeting to Mary repeat the words that come from God. In reciting the Rosary, we say these words many times. This is not a simplistic repetition. The words addressed to Mary by God himself and uttered by the divine messenger have an *inscrutable content.*

"Hail, O favored one, the Lord is with you . . ." "Blessed are you among women."

This content is closely linked to the mystery of Redemption. The words of the angel's greeting to Mary introduce this mystery, and at the same time find in it their explanation.

The first reading of the daily liturgy expresses it, which brings us to the Book of Genesis. It is there — against the background of man's first and original sin — that God announces *for the first time* the mystery of Redemption. *For the first time* he makes known his action in the future history of man and the world.

Therefore, to the tempter who is concealed in the guise of a serpent, the Creator speaks thus: *"I will put enmity between you and the woman, and between your seed and her seed; he shall bruise your head, and you shall bruise his heel."*

The words that Mary heard at the Annunciation reveal that the time has come for the fulfillment of the promise contained in the Book of Genesis. From the proto-gospel we move to the Gospel. The mystery of Redemption is about to be fulfilled. The message of the eternal God greets the "Woman": this woman is Mary of Nazareth. It greets her regarding the "seed," which she will receive from God himself: *The Holy Spirit will come upon you, and the power of the Most High will overshadow you . . ." "You will conceive in your womb and bear a son, and you shall call his name Jesus."*

Decisive words—truly. The angel's greeting to Mary constitutes the beginning of the greatest of "God's works" in the history of man and the world. This greeting opens from close up the prospect of Redemption.

It's not surprising that Mary, hearing the words of that greeting, was "troubled." The approach of the living God always inspires a holy fear. Nor is it surprising that Mary wondered *"what sort of greeting this might be."* The words of the angel placed her in front of an inscrutable divine mystery. Furthermore, they brought her into the orbit of that mystery. One cannot simply take note of the mystery. It must be meditated on again and again, and ever more profoundly. It is powerful enough to fill not only life but eternity.

And let all of us who hold dear the angel's greeting try to participate in Mary's meditation. Let us try to do it above all when we recite the Rosary.

In the words uttered by the messenger to Nazareth, Mary almost glimpses, in God, all her life on earth and its eternity.

Why, hearing that she is to become the Mother of the Son of God, does she respond not with spiritual transport but first of all with the humble *"fiat"*: "Behold, I am the handmaid of the Lord; let it be to me according to your word"?

Is it not perhaps because already at that moment she felt the piercing sorrow of the reign on the throne of David that was to be Jesus'?

At the same time the angel announces that "his kingdom will have no end."

The words of the angel's greeting to Mary begin to reveal all the Mysteries, in which the Redemption of the world will be fulfilled: the Joyful Mysteries, the Sorrowful, the Glorious. Just as in the Rosary.

Mary, who *"considered in her mind what sort of greeting this might be,"* seems to enter into all these mysteries, introducing us into them, too.

She introduces us into the mysteries of Christ and at the same time to our own mysteries. Her act of meditation at the moment of the Annunciation opens up the pathways to our meditations during the recitation of the Rosary and as a result of it.

The Rosary is the prayer through which, by repeating the angel's greeting to Mary, we seek to draw from the meditation of the Most Holy Virgin our own thoughts on the mystery of Redemption. This reflection of hers — begun at the *moment* of the Annunciation — continues into the glory of the Assumption. In eternity, Mary, deeply immersed in the Mystery of the Father, the Son, and the Holy Spirit, *joins* as our Mother the *prayer* of those who hold dear the angel's greeting and express it in the recitation of the Rosary.

In this prayer we are united with her like the Apostles gathered in the Upper Room after the Ascension of Christ. The second reading of the daily liturgy reminds us, as recorded in the Acts of the Apostles. The author — after citing the names of the individual Apostles — writes: *"All these with one accord devoted themselves to prayer, together with the women and Mary the Mother of Jesus, and with his brothers."*

With this prayer they prepared to receive the Holy Spirit, on the day of Pentecost.

Mary, who on the day of the Annunciation had received the Holy Spirit in eminent fullness, prayed with them. The special fullness of the Holy Spirit determines in her a special fullness of prayer as well. Through this singular fullness, Mary prays for us — and she prays with us.

She presides over our prayer like a mother. She brings together throughout the world the vast crowds of those who cherish the angel's greeting: they, with her, "meditate on" the Mystery of the Redemption of the world, by reciting the Rosary.

Thus the Church is continuously preparing to receive the Holy Spirit, as on the day of Pentecost.

This year is the first centenary of Pope Leo XIII's Encyclical *Supremi apostolatus,* in which the great Pope decreed that the month of October should be specially devoted to the worship of the Virgin of the Rosary. In this document, he emphasized insistently the extraordinary effectiveness which that prayer, recited with a pure and devout heart, has in obtaining from the Heavenly Father, in Christ, and through the intercession of the Mother of God, protection against the most dangerous evils that threaten Christianity and humanity itself, and in achieving the great goods of justice and peace among individuals and peoples.

With this historic gesture, Leo XIII did no more than align himself with the numerous Popes who preceded him—among them Saint Pius V—and left a legacy for those who would follow him in promoting the practice of the Rosary. For this reason, I, too, wish to say to all of you: make the Rosary the *"sweet chain that unites you to God"* by means of Mary.

I am overjoyed at being able to celebrate with you today the solemn liturgy of the Queen of the Holy Rosary. In this meaningful way we all involve ourselves in the extraordinary Jubilee of the year of Redemption.

All together let us address the Mother of God affectionately, repeating the words of the Angel Gabriel: *"Hail, O favored one, the Lord is with you . . ." "Blessed are you among women."*

And at the center of today's liturgy let us listen to Mary's response:

> *"My soul magnifies the Lord,*
> *and my spirit rejoices in God my Savior,*
> *for he has regarded the low estate of his handmaiden.*
> *For behold, henceforth all generations*
> *will call me blessed."*

OCTOBER 2, 1983

The Rosary is a true conversation with Mary

Never tire of knowing the Mother of God better and better, and above all do not tire of imitating her in her complete openness to the will of God; occupy yourselves solely with pleasing her, so that you will never make her sad.

You know it's essential to pray, and you would like to do so by recalling and considering what Jesus has done and suffered for us: the Mysteries of his infancy, of his Passion and Death, of his glorious Resurrection.

Reciting your "Mystery," or "decade," you follow the inspiration of the Holy Spirit, who, instructing you from within, leads you to imitate Jesus more closely by making you pray with Mary and, above all, like Mary. The Rosary is a great contemplative prayer, just as useful to the men and women of today, "all busy with many things"; it is the prayer of Mary and those who are devoted to her.

The Mysteries of the Rosary are justly compared to windows that you can push open and then let your gaze sink into the "world of God." It is only from that world, from the "example that Jesus left us," that you learn to be strong in trouble, patient in adversity, resolute in temptation.

You are organized into groups of fifteen, according to the number of the Mysteries of the Rosary, and you pray for one another. And so, while all of you together offer the Mother of the Redeemer the whole Crown of Hail Marys, you more easily fulfill the Word of the Lord: *"For where two or three are gathered in my name, there am I in the midst of them."*

The certainty of having Jesus with you, while you meditate on the Rosary, should make you fervent in praying to him for peace and justice for the Church and for the world, through the intercession of Our Lady.

The founder of your association, Paolina Jaricot, suggests this to you, reminding you that faith can be gained only through prayer.

But above all the Mother of the Lord suggests this to you, she who at Lourdes and especially at Fatima as a mother invited you to recite the Holy Rosary devoutly every day.

The Pope, too, encourages you in this daily recitation, for he, as you know, has made the Rosary "his favorite prayer." He encourages you above all to make yours the virtues that you recognize in the Mysteries of the Holy Rosary. Say this prayer with your friends and recite it especially in your family with the appropriate enthusiasm and persistence.

The Rosary is a true conversation with Mary, our Heavenly Mother. In the Rosary we speak to Mary so that she may intercede for us with her son Jesus. Thus we speak to God through Mary.

Dear boys and girls, you should get used to reciting the Rosary this way. It is not so much a matter of repeating formulas; rather, it is to speak as living persons with a living person, who, if you do not see her with the eyes of your body, you may, however, see with the eyes of faith. Our Lady, in fact, and her Son Jesus, live in Heaven a life much more "alive" than the mortal one that we live here on earth.

The Rosary is a confidential conversation with Mary, in which we speak to her freely and trustingly. We confide in her our troubles, reveal to her our hopes, open our hearts to her. We declare that we are at her disposal for whatever she, in the name of her Son, may ask of us. We promise faithfulness to her in every circumstance, even the most painful and difficult, sure of her protection, sure that if we ask she will obtain from her Son all the grace necessary for our salvation.

May the Holy Virgin watch over you always, dear boys and girls. May she guard you on your path, in your Christian and human development.

So, too, may she protect your parents, teachers, relatives, friends.

May she bless generously, too, the Brothers and Sisters of the ancient and glorious order of St. Dominic, who originated this devotion of the Rosary, which today is spread throughout the Church.

APRIL 25, 1987

I invite all those who are listening to me at this moment to join with me in this prayer, "so simple, yet so rich," in which we are urged to meditate on the principal episodes of the mystery of salvation as it was fulfilled in Christ: his birth and infancy; his Passion and Death; his Resurrection and Ascension; the descent of the Holy Spirit on the infant Church, and the glorification of his most pure and beloved Mother.

On October 29, 1978, a few days after my election to the Supreme Pontificate, I exhorted the faithful gathered in St. Peter's Square this way: *"The Rosary is my favorite prayer. It is a marvelous prayer! Marvelous in its simplicity and in its profundity. In this prayer we repeat over and over again the words that were spoken to the Virgin Mary by the angel and by her kinswoman Elizabeth. The entire Church shares in these words. One might say that the Rosary is, in a certain sense, a comment-prayer on the last chapter of the Constitution* Lumen Gentium *of the Second Vatican Council, a chapter that treats of the miraculous presence of the Mother of God in the mystery of Christ and the Church."*

To her, to her Immaculate Heart, I entrust you, your loved ones, Italy, the Church, all humanity, so that justice and peace may flourish.

OCTOBER 6, 1984

Queen of the Rosary, our beloved Mother

I invite you all to join spiritually in this chorus of prayer and to follow the last part of the "Petition," which I am now about to recite:

> O blessed Rosary of Mary,
> sweet chain that unites us to God,
> chain of love that unites us to the angels.
> Tower of salvation against the assaults of hell.
> Safe harbor in the universal shipwreck,
> we will never abandon you.
> You will be our comfort in the hour of death,
> to you the last kiss
> of our dying life.
> And the final word on our lips
> will be your sweet name,
> O Queen of the Rosary of Pompeii,
> O dearest Mother,
> O refuge of sinners,
> O sovereign comforter of the afflicted.
> Be everywhere blessed, today and forever,
> on earth and in Heaven.
> *Amen.*

MAY 8, 1983

The Joyful Mysteries

Mother of Christ and Mother of the Church,
we entrust and consecrate to you
the bishops, the clergy, the men and women religious,
the contemplative monks and nuns,
the seminarians, the novices.
We entrust and consecrate to you
fathers and mothers, youths, and children,
husbands and wives and those who are preparing for
marriage,
those who are called to serve
you and their neighbor in celibacy.
Help us all to work together
with a sense of the Christian ideal
and for a common Christian goal.
Help us persevere with Christ;
help us, O Mother of the Church
to construct his Mystical Body,
by living that life which he alone
can grant us from his fullness,
which is both human and divine.

SEPTEMBER 30, 1979

The Rosary elevates our feelings

The Holy Rosary is a Christian, Gospel, and ecclesial prayer, but it is also a prayer that elevates our feelings and affections.

In the Joyful Mysteries, on which we dwell briefly today, we see some of this: joy in the family, in maternity, in kinship, in friendship, in mutual aid. These are joys that sin has not annihilated, and Christ made man take them into himself and sanctified them. He achieved this through Mary. So it is through her that, even today, we can grasp the joys of man and make them our own: in themselves they are humble and simple, but in Mary and Jesus they become great and holy.

In Mary, who as a virgin was married to Joseph and who conceived by divine means, there is the joy of the chaste love of spouses and of maternity received and protected as a gift of God; in Mary, who eagerly goes to Elizabeth, there is the joy of serving our brothers by bringing to them the presence of God; in Mary, who presents to the shepherds and the Magi the long-awaited one of Israel, there is the spontaneous and trustful sharing of friendship; in Mary, who in the temple offers her own Son to the Heavenly Father, there is the anxious joy of parents and teachers for their children or students; in Mary, who after three days of anguished searching, finds Jesus, there is the painful joy of the mother who knows that her Son belongs to God before he belongs to her.

OCTOBER 23, 1983

The agony of Jesus in the garden of Gethsemane

In these Sunday meetings of ours for Marian prayer during Lent, as we journey toward Easter, we would like to pause and reflect on the Sorrowful Mysteries of the Holy Rosary. Accompanying us in our reflections is the Virgin Mary, who was an eyewitness of the culminating moment of the Passion.

We speak of *mysteries,* because they are at once *events* in the story of Jesus and *events* of our salvation. They are a *road* that Jesus traveled and travels with us so that we may experience, through conversion, communion with God and renewed brotherhood with manhood.

Today we meditate on the first Sorrowful Mystery: the agony of Jesus in the garden of Gethsemane. The evangelist and teacher of this liturgical year, St. Luke, guides us. He reports that Jesus, coming from the Last Supper, went "as usual" to the Mount of Olives. He was not alone; his Disciples, though they didn't understand, followed him. Twice, at the beginning and at the end of the event, he addressed to them the exhortation that we utter daily in the Our Father: *"Pray that you may not enter into temptation."*

This Sunday and for the next week of Lent, we welcome this divine word as a viaticum and as a genuine reminder: *"Pray that you may not enter into temptation."*

During the final trial of his life, Jesus prays in solitude: *"And he withdrew from them about a stone's throw, and knelt down and prayed."*

The content of the prayer is filial, extended into Jesus' inner agony to accept the will of the Father, faithful even in anguish for what is about to happen: *"Father, if thou art willing, remove this cup from me; nevertheless not my will, but thine, be done."*

And Jesus begins to suffer in a way that dramatically involves his whole person: *"His sweat was like drops of blood falling to the ground."* But his prayer became *"more fervent."*

Brothers and sisters, we contemplate Jesus in physical pain, in harrowing psychological and moral pain, in his abandonment and solitude, but *in prayer,* in the effort to adhere to the Father in total faithfulness.

In this season of Lent we have a precise task: *to interpret our suffering in the light of the suffering of Jesus*— experienced in grief and compassion — and to pray, to pray more and more.

Prayer in the privacy of our room; prayer in offering our work; prayer in listening to and meditating on the Word of God; prayer in the family through the Holy Rosary; liturgical prayer, the source and culmination of our inner life.

Most Holy Mary teaches us both to accept suffering in an attitude of obedient love and to elevate our soul to God through daily prayer. Especially during this time of Lent, we want to enroll ourselves, as attentive disciples, in her school.

FEBRUARY 12, 1989

Jesus is scourged

In the Marian prayer of the second Sunday of Lent, let us reflect on the second sorrowful mystery of the Rosary: Jesus is scourged.

The Gospel of St. Luke emphasizes three times the tortures that Jesus suffered before he was put to death.

First of all, before his appearance at the Sanhedrin: *"Now the men who were holding Jesus mocked him and beat him; they also blindfolded him and asked him, 'Prophesy! Who is it that struck you?' And they spoke many other words against him, reviling him."* He who more than anyone else deserved to be called *prophet*—that is, one who speaks in the name and with the power of God—is mocked because of what for him is the most profound personal reality: being the Word of God.

An analogous scene is repeated in the encounter with Herod Antipas: *"And Herod with his soldiers treated him with contempt and mocked him; then, arraying him in gorgeous apparel, he sent him back to Pilate."*

And when Jesus comes before Pilate, Luke notes, for the third time: *"Pilate said: . . . I will therefore chastise him and release him."*

St. Mark describes this punishment: "So Pilate, wishing to satisfy the crowd, released for them Barabbas; and *having scourged Jesus,* he delivered him to be crucified."

The Roman *flagellatio,* or scourging, carried out by soldiers equipped with the *flagellum,* or *flagrum,* a whip made of knotted leather cords, or bearing at the end a blunt instrument, was the punishment reserved for slaves and those condemned to death. Its effects were terrible: those upon whom it was inflicted often died under the lashes.

Jesus would not spare himself even this horrific suffering: he confronted it for us.

Meditating on this second sorrowful mystery of the Rosary, we hear ourselves called to be disciples of Jesus in his suffering. He prayed for us also with *his body,* subjecting it to unspeakable tortures in obedience to the plan of the Father. He gave himself to the

Father and to men, manifesting to all of us unfathomable human misery and the extraordinary possibility of renewal and salvation, which is given to us in him.

On the example of Jesus, we, too, must pray with our bodies. The choices that require demanding and difficult behavior, such as chastity according to one's state of life, giving assistance to our brothers and sisters, and other physically tiring activities, become prayer and sacrifice to be offered to God in a redemptive union with the "sufferings of Christ."

We therefore accept the "scourge" that personal sobriety and the exercise of Christian charity, every day, make us experience. It is the fruit and gift of the sorrowful mystery of Jesus, which spurs us on, involves us, transforms us inwardly.

May the Virgin of Sorrows lighten our task with her intercession.

FEBRUARY 19, 1989

Jesus is crowned with thorns

Let us devote today's meeting for the Marian prayer to the contemplation of the third sorrowful mystery: the crowning of Jesus with thorns.

The moment is attested to by the Gospels, which, though they do not dwell on many details, point out the acts of aggression and the insane enjoyment of Pilate's soldiers.

"And the soldiers," Mark writes, followed by Matthew and John, *"led him away inside the palace (that is, the praetorium); and they called together the whole battalion. And they clothed him in a purple cloak, and plaiting a crown of thorns they put it on him. And they began to salute him, 'Hail, King of the Jews!' And they struck his head with a reed, and spat upon him, and they knelt down in homage to him."*

Matthew adds only one detail: a mocking symbol of royalty: first they place the reed in Jesus' right hand, like a royal scepter, then they take it away from him and beat him on the head with it.

We have before us an image of sorrow, which evokes all the homicidal madness, all the sadism of history. Jesus, too, wanted to be at the mercy of the sometimes extraordinarily cruel wickedness of men.

John induces us to transform our contemplation into worshipful and anxious prayer before the suffering of Jesus crowned with thorns: *"Pilate,"* he writes, *"went out again, and said to them, 'See, I am bringing him out to you, that you may know that I find no crime in him.' So Jesus came out, wearing the crown of thorns and the purple robe, Pilate said to them, 'Behold the man!' "*

Truly that Man is the Son of God, who, through unspeakable suffering, brings to fulfillment the Father's plan of salvation. He has grasped our sorrows so deeply that he shares them, assumes them, gives them meaning, transforms them into an unhoped-for possibility of life, grace, and communion with God and hence glory.

From that day, every human generation has been called to declare itself before that "man" crowned with thorns. No one can remain neutral. One must declare oneself. And not only with words but with one's life.

The Christian accepts the crown of thorns on his head, when he knows how to mortify his arrogance, his pride, the various forms of selfishness and hedonism, which end up destroying him as a person and often lead him to be cruel to others.

Lent invites each of us to enter on the path of liberation from whatever slavery torments us. Our King, the Man-God, is before us: he gives us new heart, so that we may experience our anxiety and our suffering in a form that leads to salvation, through his love and love of our brothers.

The Most Holy Virgin precedes us on this difficult path and encourages us to quicken our steps, pointing out to us the radiant goal of Easter.

FEBRUARY 26, 1989

Jesus on the road to Calvary

In our Lent meeting for the Marian prayer of the Angelus our thoughts turn to the fourth sorrowful mystery of the Holy Rosary: Jesus on the road to Calvary.

Our meditation will emphasize in particular the fact that determined that anguished journey: Jesus' condemnation to death. St. Luke writes: *"The chief priests, the rulers and the people . . . demanded that he be crucified . . . he [Pilate] delivered up Jesus to their will."*

"Hand over," "deliver," "handed over" are terms that recur in the story. They are translations of the Latin *tradere* and *traditum,* words that reflect both Pilate's act of cowardice and the plan of the Father and the loving will of the Son, who accepts "being delivered up" for the salvation of the world.

Along the Via Dolorosa the evangelist St. Luke offers us, then, models that teach us to live, in our daily life, the Passion of Jesus as the road to Resurrection.

The first example is Simon of Cyrene, *"who was coming in from the country, and [they] laid on him the cross, to carry it behind Jesus."* It is not only carrying the Cross that is relevant. Many individuals in the world suffer terribly: every people, every family has sorrows and burdens to bear. What gives fullness of meaning to the Cross is that Simon carries it behind Jesus, not on a path of anguished solitude or rebellion but on a path sustained and vivified by the divine presence of the Lord.

The second example consists of the *"great multitude of the people, and of women who bewailed and lamented him [Jesus]."* Compassionate words and even shared tears are not sufficient: we must be cognizant of our own responsibility in the drama of sorrow, especially when it is innocent. That leads us to make a useful contribution to its alleviation.

Jesus' words do not indulge in a sterile sentimentality but invite us to a realistic reading of the history of individuals and communities. *"For if they do this when the wood is green, what will happen when it is dry?"* If the supremely innocent man is abused in this way, what will happen to those who are responsible for the evil that has taken place in the history of individuals and nations?

Jesus' sorrowful journey, the Via Crucis, the Way of the Cross, is a precious reminder to us to recognize the value of our daily suffering; a lesson not to avoid it with opportunistic pretexts or vain excuses; an impetus to make of it instead a gift to him who loved us, in the certainty that in this way we will build a new culture of love and cooperate in the divine work of salvation.

May Mary, who with the other women, followed Jesus on the way of the Cross, and whom we will find on Calvary, be for us a model in this gift of ourselves: may she help us to understand the value of our suffering and offer it to the Father joined with Christ's suffering.

MARCH 5, 1989

Jesus dies on the Cross

On this fifth Sunday of Lent, at the hour of Marian prayer, let us reflect on the fifth sorrowful mystery of the Holy Rosary: Jesus dies on the Cross.

The Crucifixion and Death of Jesus join together Heaven and earth, just as the other fundamental events of the story of salvation do: the creation, the birth of Jesus, the Resurrection, the final coming, or Parousia, of the Lord. The evangelist Luke writes: *"It was now about the sixth hour, and there was darkness over the whole land until the ninth hour, while the sun's light failed."*

This event expresses with stunning clarity how Jesus is a symbol of contradiction. In fact, people line up on two sides: those who know him and adore him; and those who mock him.

St. Luke leads us on to contemplate Jesus in prayer: *"Father, forgive them, for they know not what they do."* It is the most sublime school of love: in sorrow, Jesus tries to forgive those who have made him suffer, responding to evil with good. St. Stephen, the first Christian martyr, will repeat this prayer of Jesus'.

"The rulers" and *"the soldiers,"* disappointed in their expectations, mock Jesus. The people, on the other hand, *"stood by, watching."* The two *"criminals"* also display contradictory attitudes. While one insults him, the other is testimony of an extraordinary experience of reconciliation: he recognizes his own condition as a sinner, which differentiates him radically from the man who is suffering beside him (*"But this man has done nothing wrong"*), and entrusts himself fully to the love of Jesus.

St. John then shows us Mary at the foot of the Cross: a woman of sorrow, which is offered through love; the woman of giving and acceptance; the Mother of Jesus; the Mother of the Church; the Mother of all men.

There were other women, too, near the Cross, but Jesus, *"when he saw his mother, and the disciple whom he loved standing near,"* utters words that have a profound spiritual resonance: *"Woman, behold, your son"*; *"Behold, your mother."* In John every man discovers that he is the son of the mother who gave to the world the Son of God.

At the moment of death Jesus prays, proclaiming his ultimate *gift* to the Father for the salvation of all men: *"Father, into thy hands I commit my spirit."*

Confronting the mystery of Christ who dies to save us, let us, too, say: *"Truly this man is the Son of God."*

May the Virgin Mary help us in our commitment to the road of faith as we approach the holy days, in worshipful silence, in full willingness to make our life, our particular story, a gift to share, in love and hope, with our brothers.

MARCH 12, 1989

Mary is the model of the victorious Church

In the Glorious Mysteries of the Holy Rosary the hopes of the Christian are relived: the hopes of eternal life, which engage God's omnipotence, and the expectations of the present time, which commit men to work with God.

In Christ who rises all the world rises, and there will begin a new Heaven and a new earth, which will be fulfilled at his glorious return, when *"death shall be no more, neither shall there be mourning nor crying nor pain anymore, for the former things have passed away."*

In him who ascends to Heaven human nature is exalted, placed on the right hand of God, and the order to evangelize the world is given to the Disciples; further, in ascending to Heaven, Christ was not taken from the earth: he is concealed in the face of every man and woman, especially the unfortunate: the poor, the ill, the marginalized, the persecuted . . .

Pouring out the Holy Spirit at Pentecost, he gave the Disciples the strength to love and to spread his truth; he asked for a community that would build a world worthy of man who has been redeemed; and he granted the capacity to sanctify all things in obedience to the will of the Heavenly Father. In this way he rekindled the joy of giving in those who give, and the certainty of being loved in the hearts of the unhappy.

In the glory of the Virgin assumed into Heaven, the first to be redeemed, we contemplate, among other things, the true sublimation of the ties of blood and family affections: Christ glorified Mary not only because she is Immaculate, the ark of the divine presence, but also because, as a Son, he honors his Mother: the holy bonds of earth do not break in Heaven. Rather, in the solicitude of the Virgin Mother, assumed into Heaven to become our advocate and protector, the model of the victorious Church, we can see the same inspiring example of the attentive love of our beloved dead toward us, not broken by death but made powerful in the light of God.

Finally, in the vision of Mary glorified by all creatures, we celebrate the eschatological mystery of a humanity remade in Christ in perfect unity, with no more divisions, without rivalry, so that one is not ahead of another in love. Because God is Love.

In the Mysteries of the Holy Rosary we contemplate and relive the joys, the sorrows, and the glories of Christ and his Holy Mother, which become the joys, the sorrows, and the hopes of mankind.

NOVEMBER 6, 1983

Extend your protection over all the earth

With the simplicity and fervor of St. Bernadette let us recite the Holy Rosary!

First decade:
Let us honor the Resurrection of the Lord Jesus.
— Let us bless the Mother of the victor over death and sin.
— With her, let us bless the risen Christ.
— Let us pray to Mary to strengthen the faith of Christian communities and of the entire world.

Second decade:
Let us honor the exaltation of Christ in the divine glory, the Mystery of the Ascension:
— Let us rejoice with Our Lady at the heavenly glorification of her Son.
— Let us praise Christ, the new Adam, for restoring to men the destiny of immortality and life with God.
— Let us entrust to Mary the individuals and peoples who have lost or who do not know or who fight Christian hope.

Third decade:
Let us celebrate Pentecost.
— Let us praise Mary, in whom the Holy Spirit has given life to the Redeemer of the world.
— Let us praise Jesus who poured out his Spirit on the first Disciples, as he does on those of today.
— Let us entreat Mary, true to the Spirit, to grant this fidelity to the leaders and the members of the Church.

Fourth decade:
Let us honor the Assumption of the Virgin Mary.

— Let us praise Mary of Nazareth, Mary of Bethlehem, of the presentation in the temple, of Cana, of Calvary, of the Upper Room: she was glorified immediately in body and soul.
— Let us thank Jesus for enabling his Mother to share in his life as the Risen one.
— Let us pray to Mary that she may give us the joy and hope of joining her.

Fifth decade:
Let us honor the glorification of Our Lady.
— Let us hail Mary, in keeping with the tradition of the Church, who shares in the spiritual sovereignty of Christ the Redeemer.
— Let us bless Jesus who wished to unite his Mother to the expansion of his Kingdom!
O Mother of the Church,
O Queen of the universe,
we pray to you:
extend over all the earth.
your motherly protection!

AUGUST 14, 1983

Rosary for peace
Prayer, stronger than any weapon

Brothers and sisters,

Our hearts are full of sorrow because of the war going on in the Gulf region, from which day after day news reaches us that is more and more distressing, about the number of combatants and the number of weapons, and the involvement of whole civilian populations.

What makes this even more worrying is the risk that this discouraging picture may extend in both time and space, with tragic and incalculable consequences.

As men and women and as Christians, we must not get used to the idea that this is all unavoidable, and we must not let our souls yield to the temptation of indifference and fatalistic resignation, as if men couldn't help being caught in the spiral of war.

As believers in the God of mercy and in his Son Jesus, who died and rose for the salvation of all, we cannot give up hope that this tremendous suffering, which involves such a large number of people, will end as soon as possible. To achieve this goal, we have at our disposal in the first place prayer, a humble instrument but, if nurtured with sincere and intense faith, stronger than any weapon and any human calculation. We entrust to God our profound sorrow together with our most vivid hope.

Let us call on the divine light for those who, in international spheres, continue to seek ways of peace; who, making efforts to end the war, have a desire for peace and justice, and a strong will to find adequate solutions to the various problems of the Middle East.

We ask the Lord to enlighten the leaders on all sides of the conflict, so that they may find the courage to abandon the road of warlike confrontation, and to trust, sincerely, in negotiation, dialogue, and collaboration.

We ask divine comfort for all those who suffer on account of war and the serious problems of injustice and insecurity that have not yet been solved in the region of the Middle East.

In this trustful appeal to divine mercy, I exhort you all to be in harmony with other believers, above all with the peoples of Jewish, Christian, and Muslim faiths, who are most stricken by this war.

By reciting the Rosary and meditating on the mysteries of Christ, we place our sorrow, our worries, and our hopes in the Immaculate Heart of Mary, our Mother.

FEBRUARY 2, 1991

Meditation on the Mysteries of the Rosary

First Mystery
THE ANNUNCIATION
*In the womb of the Virgin Mary, the Word of God
became man to reconcile man with God.*

WORD OF THE LORD
From the Gospel according to Luke (1:28, 31–33).

The angel came to her and said: "Hail, O favored one, the Lord is with you. . . . Behold, you will conceive in your womb and bear a son, and you shall call his name Jesus. . . . The Lord God will give to him the throne of his father David and he will reign over the house of Jacob forever; and of his kingdom there will be no end."

TEACHING OF THE CHURCH
*From the radio message to the world of
Pope Pius XII (August 24, 2939).*

"It is by the force of reason, not of arms, that justice advances. And empires not founded on justice are not blessed by God. . . . Nothing is lost with peace. Everything can be lost with war. Let men return to understanding one another. Let them begin to negotiate again. If they can negotiate with goodwill and respect for mutual rights, they will realize that sincere, useful dialogue never rules out an honorable conclusion."

— Our Father
— Hail Mary
— Glory Be

PRAYER

Lord,
who are the source of justice and the origin of harmony,
in the angel's announcement to Mary
you brought men the good news
of reconciliation between Heaven and earth:
open men's hearts to dialogue
and support the task of those who work for peace,
so that negotiation will prevail over recourse to arms,
understanding over incomprehension,
forgiveness over offense,
love over hate.
Through Christ our Lord.
Amen.

Second Mystery
THE BIRTH OF JESUS IN BETHLEHEM
With the birth of the Son of the Virgin
the gift of peace is offered to all men, near and far.

WORD OF THE LORD
From the Gospel according to Luke (2:11, 13–14).

The angel said to the shepherds: "To you is born this day in the city of David a savior, who is Christ the Lord." And suddenly there was with the angel a multitude of the heavenly host praising God and saying, "Glory to God in the highest and on earth peace among men with whom he is pleased."

TEACHING OF THE CHURCH
From the Encyclical Pacem in Terris *of Pope John XXIII*
(April 11, 1963, No. 60).

"This is the peace that we ask of the Lord Jesus with the burning breath of our prayer. May he remove from the hearts of men that which endangers it; and may he transform them into witnesses of truth, justice, and brotherly love.

"May he enlighten the leaders of peoples, so that, in addition to their care for the proper well-being of their citizens, they may guarantee and defend the great gift of peace; may he inspire in all men the will to overcome the barriers that divide them, to increase the bonds of mutual charity, to understand others, to forgive those who have brought injustices; by virtue of his action, may all the peoples of the earth become brothers and may the much longed-for peace flourish among them and reign forever."

— Our Father
— Hail Mary
— Glory Be

PRAYER

God of our Fathers
Father of all,
who in your Son Jesus, the Prince of Peace,
give true peace to people near and far,
hear the petition that the Church addresses to you
together with the Mother of your Son:
help the soldiers on every front
who, forced by grievous decisions,
are fighting one another in the Gulf War;
free them from feelings of hatred and revenge,
enable them to keep in their hearts
the desire for peace,
so that when they are faced with the horrors of war
distress does not become for them
depression and desperation.
Through Christ our Lord.
Amen.

Third Mystery
THE DEATH OF JESUS ON THE CROSS
*With the death of Jesus every dividing wall was knocked down
and there was peace among peoples.*

WORD OF THE LORD
From the Gospel according to John (19:28–30).

Jesus, knowing that all was now finished, said (to fulfill the Scripture), "I thirst.". . . When Jesus had received the vinegar he said, "It is finished!" And he bowed his head and gave up his spirit.

TEACHING OF THE CHURCH
From the Pastoral Constitution Gaudium et Spes
of the Second Vatican Council (December 7, 1965, No. 78).

"That earthly peace which arises from love of neighbor symbolizes and results from the peace of Christ which radiates from God the Father. For by the Cross the Incarnate Son, the Prince of Peace, reconciled all men with God. By thus restoring all men to the unity of one people and one body, he slew hatred in his own flesh. . . .

"For this reason, all Christians are urgently summoned to do in love what the truth requires, and to join with all true peacemakers in pleading for peace and bringing it about."

— Our Father
— Hail Mary
— Glory Be

PRAYER
Father,
your Son, the Holy, the innocent,
died on the Cross,
a victim of man's sin.

He died
soaking the earth with blood
and sowing in the hearts of men
words of forgiveness and peace.
Hear. O Father,
the cry of innocent blood
spilled on the battlefields,
and welcome into your dwelling of light,
through the maternal intercession of the Mother of
   sorrow,
those men whom the violence of weapons
has torn from life
and delivered into the hands of your mercy.
Through Christ our Lord.
Amen.

Fourth Mystery

THE RESURRECTION OF JESUS

In the Resurrection of Christ
peace is communicated
to mankind and all creatures.

WORD OF THE LORD

From the Gospel according to John (20:19–21).

On the evening of that day, the first day of the week . . . Jesus came
and stood among his Disciples and said to them, "Peace be with
you!" Then the Disciples were glad when they saw the Lord. Jesus
said to them again, "Peace be with you!"

TEACHING OF THE CHURCH

From the speech of Pope Paul VI to the General Assembly
of the United Nations (October 4, 1965, No.5).

"You are waiting for this word from us, which cannot but be clothed in gravity and solemnity: *never again one against another,* never, never again!

"It was principally for this purpose that the United Nations came into being: against war and for peace. . . .

"It doesn't take many words to state the highest goal of this institution. We need only recall that the blood of millions of people and innumerable and unprecedented sufferings, useless slaughter and tremendous ruin ratify the pact that unites you, with an oath that must change the future history of the world: never again war, never again war!

"Peace, peace must guide the fate of peoples and of all humanity."

— Our Father
— Hail Mary
— Glory Be

PRAYER

Father, you who love life,
who in the Resurrection of your Son Jesus
have renewed man and all creation
and wish to bring them
peace as your first gift:
look with compassion
upon humanity torn apart by war;
save the creatures
of the sky, the earth, and the sea,
the work of your hands,

threatened by destruction among unprecedented sufferings,
and let peace alone, through the intercession of Holy Mary,
guide the fate
of peoples and of nations.
Through Jesus Christ our Lord.
Amen.

Fifth Mystery
THE DESCENT OF THE HOLY SPIRIT
*At Pentecost, the Spirit of God, the Spirit of peace and harmony,
was poured out over all peoples.*

WORD OF THE LORD
From the Acts of the Apostles (2:1, 4, 6, 9–11).

When the day of Pentecost had come . . . the Disciples were all
filled with the Holy Spirit and began to speak in other tongues. . . .
And the multitude were bewildered because each one heard them
speaking in his own language. . . .

Parthians and Medes and Elamites, and residents of
Mesopotamia, Judea and Cappadocia, Pontus and Asia, Phrygia
and Pamphylia, Egypt and the parts of Libya belonging to Cyrene,
and visitors from Rome, both Jews and proselytes, Cretans and
Arabians, we hear them telling in our own tongues the mighty
works of God.

TEACHING OF THE CHURCH
From the Message Urbi et Orbi *of Pope John Paul II (Christmas, 1990).*

"The light of Christ shines on the tormented nations of the Middle East. Fearfully we wait for the threat of war to vanish from the
region of the Gulf.

"Convince the leaders that war is an adventure that has no return! With reason, patience, and dialogue, and with respect for the inalienable rights of populations and peoples, it is possible that we may discover the pathways of understanding and peace, and follow them.

"The Holy Land, too, has been waiting many years for peace: a peaceful solution to the entire question that vexes it, a solution that takes account of the legitimate expectations of the Palestinian people and of those who live in the state of Israel."

— Our Father
— Hail Mary
— Glory Be

PRAYER

In this time of unprecedented violence
and useless slaughter,
hear, O Father,
the entreaty that goes up to you from all the Church,
as we pray with Mary, Queen of Peace:
instill in the governments of all nations
the Spirit of unity and harmony,
of love and peace,
so that the hoped-for message
may reach the ends of the earth:
War is over!
And, with the clash of arms silenced,
may hymns of peace and brotherhood echo throughout
    the earth.
Through Christ our Lord.
Amen.

— Salve Regina
— Litanies

Prayer for Peace

God of our Fathers,
mighty and merciful,
Lord of peace and life,
Father of all.

You have plans for peace, not violence,
you condemn war
and overthrow the pride of the aggressor.

You sent your Son Jesus
to declare peace near and far,
to unite men of every race and every creed
in a single family.
Hear the unanimous cry of your children,
the heartfelt petition of all humanity:
no more war, an adventure without return,
no more war, a spiral of grief and violence;
stop this war in the Persian Gulf,
this threat to your creatures
in the sky, on earth, and in the sea.

In communion with Mary, the Mother of Jesus,
again we entreat you:
speak to the hearts of those responsible for the fate
    of peoples,
stop the logic of reprisal and revenge,
through your Spirit suggest new solutions,
generous and honorable gestures,
space for dialogue and patient waiting:

more fruitful than the frenzied descent into war.
Grant in our time
days of peace.
No more war.
Amen.

February 2, 1991

From the Encyclical Redemptoris Mater
of John Paul II (No. 40)

TEACHING OF THE CHURCH

After the events of the Resurrection and Ascension, Mary entered the Upper Room together with the Apostles to await Pentecost, and was present there as the Mother of the glorified Lord. She was not only the one who "advanced in her pilgrimage of faith" and loyally persevered in her union with her Son "unto the Cross," but she was also the "handmaid of the Lord," left by her Son as Mother in the midst of the infant Church: "Behold your mother." After her Son's departure, her motherhood remains in the Church as mediator: interceding for all her children, the Mother cooperates in the saving work of her Son, the Redeemer of the world.

— Our Father
— Hail Mary
— Glory Be

PRAYER

Almighty God,
lover of life,
we, like the Apostles on the day of Pentecost,
are in prayerful communion
with Mary, the Mother of your Son;
as supplicants we ask you
to renew in all and in each
the gifts of the Consoler,
so that, comforted by his presence,
we may proclaim your mercy

and communicate it with our lives
to all creatures.
Through Christ our Lord.
Amen.

Meditation

In reciting the Rosary, we have repeated with faith the words of the angel, *"Hail Mary,"* and of St. Elizabeth, *"Blessed are you among women,"* reliving the same attitude of loving trust that your forebears had toward her, the Mother of the Redeemer. In difficult and sometimes tragic situations, in times of catastrophe, invasion, and war, they were able to find, in their faith in God the Father, in Jesus Christ the Redeemer, and in the Holy Spirit, love, the foundation of fearless strength, which sustained them, nourishing their hope in unfailing divine intervention.

In every *Hail Mary* they recalled the mysterious gift made by God to man, to every man, in the Incarnation of the Word, and they knew very well that the condition of this mortal life can find support and protection in the Mother of God, since it is Mary who gave the Savior to the world, and who with boundless affection prays for us sinners *"now and in the hour of our death."*

Like them, we, too, in the *Hail Mary,* this simple prayer that children learn on their mother's knee, call on the Virgin full of grace, we entrust ourselves to her intercession, we bless her divine Son, the fruit of her womb, echoing the words of the Gospel: *"Blessed is the womb that bore you, the breast that suckled you."* We declare, similarly, that her maternal aid is indispensable to us at the fundamental moments of our existence: in the present and in the "hour of our death," the decisive moment of passage to eternal life.

These simple considerations offer us the opportunity to reflect briefly on the importance of prayer: public and liturgical, private, personal, and familial; the prayer that we say aloud, repeating ancient and venerable words, and the one that goes silently up from the heart, accompanied by the most profound emotions of our soul.

The Rosary, in a special way, with its meditations on the mysteries, engages one's full expressive capacity in oral prayer. As we relive the moments of joy and sorrow in the life of Christ and his Immaculate Mother, our spirit is nourished, which leads us to dialogue with the Lord and to contemplation. In the Rosary we also recall our human condition marked by sin and ask for divine forgiveness. We ask for the graces that we need: first of all that we may escape evil and live in friendship with the Lord, in accordance with his Gospel. The life of the Redeemer, miraculously marked by the power of the Father and the living presence of the Holy Spirit, appears to us, through the Joyful, Sorrowful, and Glorious Mysteries, as the model of our baptismal vocation, directed to the imitation and following of the divine Teacher.

The Marian prayer, then, is an interior pilgrimage that leads the believer, with the help of the Virgin, to the spiritual mountain of holiness. It is the school of ecclesial communion, in the hearing of the one who occupies in the Church the place that is highest and closest to Christ. Mary is the model of hardworking charity, since, "embracing with all her soul and with no burden of sin the saving will of God, she devoted herself completely as the handmaid of the Lord to the person and the work of her Son, helping in the mystery of Redemption dependent on him and with him, by the grace of Almighty God." Mary is the image and the origin of the Church, and she remains vitally joined to it through her communion with the Redeemer. We cannot, therefore, think of living in true devotion to Our Lady if we are not in full harmony with the Church and its Bishop. If we do not take care to be, at the same time, an obedient child of the Church, whose duty it is to verify the legitimacy of the various forms of religious feeling, we would be deluding ourselves that she hears us as her child. It is not by chance that the Second Vatican Council warned, with all the solemnity of its teaching authority, "The faithful must remember that true devotion does not consist in a sterile and transient feeling, or in a secure yet vain credulity, but, rather, proceeds from true faith."

Dear brothers and sisters, as your fathers, more than five hundred years ago, climbed this Hill as penitents, aware of their own misery but exultant because they had been assured by their Bishop of the merciful intercession of Mary, so, too, we have now come to the foot of it, inspired by our great trust. "Mary is present in the Church as the Mother of Christ . . . and embraces with her new maternity in the Spirit all and each of us in the Church, embraces all and each of us through the Church."

"Show thyself a Mother," your fathers wrote under the image of Our Lady of Mount Berico.* "Show thyself a Mother," we, too, repeat, affectionately, conscious of the deep bond that exists between the Mother of Christ and the Church, between love for Christ and love for the Church. As we know, Mary, who was "present in the mystery of Christ, is constantly present in the mystery of the Church as well." Comforted by that truth, we wish to be, in turn, her devoted children, by remaining faithful children of the Church, in line with the Christian generations that have preceded us. We wish to love Mary in the present and in eternal life.

O Mary,
turn your merciful gaze toward us.
Show thyself a mother!
Show thyself the mother of those who suffer
and long for justice and peace.

---

*The shrine of Our Lady of Mount Berico is on a hill outside Vicenza. It is a place of Marian devotion and pilgrimage, kept by the Friar Servants of Mary.

"Show thyself the mother of every man
who struggles for the life that does not die.
Mother of humanity
redeemed by the blood of Christ:
Mother of perfect love,
of hope and peace,
Holy Mother of the Redeemer."
Show thyself our mother,
the mother of unity and hope,
while with the whole Church we cry out to you again:
"Mother of mercy,
our life, our sweetness, and our hope...
after this our exile show unto us
the blessed fruit of your womb, Jesus!
O clement, O loving,
O sweet Virgin Mary."

Rosary for vocations

The Joyful Mysteries
THE VOCATION OF MARY

1. The Annunciation (Luke 1:26–38)
Mary's "yes" was above all an act of generosity, not only toward God but also toward men and women.

Let us pray: that children and young people may be attentive and generous to God's calls.

2. The Visitation (Luke 1:39–45)
Mary's gesture of putting herself "at the service of" Elizabeth was the result of her "yes" to God.

Let us pray: that the testimony of the permanent deacons and the consecrated in the secular institutes may be fruitful.

3. The Nativity (Luke 2:1–7)
God became man so that man might become like God. He is our brother in joy and sorrow.

Let us pray: for all those who offer their lives to share the lives of the poorest.

4. The Presentation in the Temple (Luke 2:22–35)
Parents who offer a child to God do not lose him, except to find him again transformed and enriched by grace.

Let us pray: that Christian families may be generous and open to every vocation.

5. The Finding (Luke 2:41–52)
The plans of the Lord are at times difficult to understand; they require acceptance, faith, and humility.

Let us pray: for the seminarians who are preparing for consecration.

The Sorrowful Mysteries
THE VOCATION OF JESUS

1. The Agony in the Garden (Luke 22:40–44)
Even at the time of our hardest trials, the Father waits and supports our "yes" to his will.

Let us pray: that the Father may give the gift of perseverance to those who have consecrated themselves to him entirely.

2. The Scourging (Mark 15:11–15)
Faithfulness to our vocation is needed to overcome others' lack of understanding and their attempts to discourage us.

Let us pray: for those who suffer persecution because of the Gospel.

3. The Crown of Thorns (Mark 15:17–20)
Sometimes suffering becomes part of our life as a true vocation.

Let us pray: that the sick will unite their suffering to the redeeming Passion of Christ.

4. The Condemnation to Death (John 19:13–16)
Often, the circumstances of life are a call from God to share the journey of our brothers.

Let us pray: that every Christian may feel responsible for the salvation of the world.

5. Crucifixion and Death (John 19:28–30)
If someone wants to follow Christ, he must renounce himself and take up the cross.

Let us pray: that men and women religious and those who live a contemplative life will adhere fully to their consecration.

The Glorious Mysteries
THE VOCATION OF THE CHURCH

1. The Resurrection (Mark 16:9–14)
Today, as he was yesterday and always will be, he is the Risen One, the God of life and joy, to whom we are all called.

Let us pray: that Christian spouses may live God's love and be open to the gift of life.

2. The Ascension (Mark 16:15–19)

God needs our help to construct a world according to the Gospel.

Let us pray: that the priests in the Church may be numerous and holy.

3. The Pentecost (Acts 1:14, 2:2–4)

The Holy Spirit in us is the strength and courage to defend and spread the message of the Gospel.

Let us pray: that, through the testimony of missionaries, the missionary zeal of the Church may be constantly renewed.

4. The Assumption of Mary (Apocalypse 12:1)

Our earthly life, lived in faith, is destined for the glory of Heaven.

Let us pray: that those who are disappointed by life may find Christian hope.

5. The Crowning of Mary (Luke 1:30–33)

Even today Mary intercedes for our bewildered world and for the urgent needs of the Church.

Let us pray: that the Kingdom of God may be fulfilled.

Prayer for lay people

O Most Blessed Virgin Mary,
Mother of Christ and Mother of the Church,
With joy and wonder we seek to make our own
your Magnificat, joining you in
your hymn of thankfulness and love.

With you we give thanks to God,
"whose mercy
is from generation to generation,"
for the exalted vocation
and the many forms of mission
entrusted to the lay faithful.
God has called each of them by name
to live his own communion of love
and holiness
and to be one
in the great family of God's children.
He has sent them forth
to shine with the light of Christ
and to communicate the fire of the Spirit
in every part of society
through their life
inspired by the Gospel.

O Virgin of the Magnificat,
fill their hearts
with gratitude and enthusiasm
for this vocation and mission.

With humility and magnanimity
you were the "handmaid of the Lord";

give us your unreserved willingness
for service to God
and the salvation of the world.
Open our eyes
to the great anticipation
of the Kingdom of God
and of the proclamation of the Gospel
to the whole of creation.

Your mother's heart
is ever mindful of the many dangers
and evils which threaten
to overpower men and women
in our time.
At the same time your heart also takes notice
of the many initiatives
undertaken for good,
the great yearning for values,
and the progress achieved
in bringing forth
the abundant fruits of salvation.

O Virgin full of courage,
may your spiritual strength
and trust in God inspire us,
so that we might know
how to overcome all the obstacles
that we encounter
in accomplishing our mission.
Teach us to treat the affairs
of the world
with a real sense of Christian responsibility
and a joyful hope
of the coming of God's Kingdom, and
of a "new Heaven and a new earth."

You who were together in prayer
with the Apostles in the Upper Room,
awaiting the coming
of the Spirit at Pentecost,
implore his renewed outpouring
on all the faithful, men and women alike,
so that they may more fully respond
to their vocation and mission,
as branches engrafted to the true vine,
called to bear much fruit
for the life of the world.

O Virgin Mother,
guide and sustain us
so that we may always live
as true sons and daughters
of the Church of your Son.
Enable us to do our part
in helping to establish on earth
the civilization of truth and love,
as God wills it,
for his glory.
Amen.

CHRISTIFIDELIS LAICI
(APOSTOLIC EXHORTATION,
DECEMBER 30, 1988)

Litany prayer

Lord, have mercy	Lord, have mercy
Christ, have mercy	Christ, have mercy
Lord, have mercy	Lord, have mercy
Holy Mary	pray for us
Holy Mother of God	pray for us
Holy Virgin of virgins	pray for us
Daughter beloved of the Father	pray for us
Mother of Christ, King of the Ages	pray for us
Glory of the Holy Spirit	pray for us
Virgin daughter of Zion	pray for us
Virgin poor and humble	pray for us
Virgin meek and mild	pray for us
Servant obedient in faith	pray for us
Mother of the Lord	pray for us
Cooperator of the Redeemer	pray for us
Full of grace	pray for us
Source of beauty	pray for us
Treasure of virtue and wisdom	pray for us
First fruit of the Redemption	pray for us
Perfect disciple of Christ	pray for us
Purest image of the Church	pray for us

Woman of the new covenant	pray for us
Woman clothed in sun	pray for us
Woman crowned with stars	pray for us
Lady of immense bounty	pray for us
Lady of forgiveness	pray for us
Lady of our families	pray for us
Joy of the new Israel	pray for us
Splendor of the Holy Church	pray for us
Honor of the human race	pray for us
Advocate of grace	pray for us
Minister of divine mercy	pray for us
Help of God's people	pray for us
Queen of love	pray for us
Queen of mercy	pray for us
Queen of peace	pray for us
Queen of the angels	pray for us
Queen of the patriarchs	pray for us
Queen of the prophets	pray for us
Queen of the Apostles	pray for us
Queen of the martyrs	pray for us
Queen of the confessors of the faith	pray for us
Queen of virgins	pray for us
Queen of all the saints	pray for us
Queen conceived without sin	pray for us
Queen assumed into Heaven	pray for us
Queen of the earth	pray for us
Queen of Heaven	pray for us
Queen of the universe	pray for us

Lamb of God
who take away the sins of the world, forgive us, Lord.
Lamb of God
who take away the sins of the world, hear us, Lord.
Lamb of God
who take away the sins of the world, have pity on us.

Pray for us, glorious Mother of the Lord.
Make us worthy of Christ's promises.

Merciful God,
hear the prayer of your people
who honor with solemn rites
the Blessed Virgin Mary, your servant,
as mother and queen.,
and grant that we may serve you and our brothers
in this world
to enter into the eternal dwelling of your kingdom.
Through Christ our Lord.
Amen.

Conclusion

I would like to make many recommendations,
but I will leave you with one that is essential:
continue to love the Holy Rosary
and spread its practice
wherever you happen to be.

It is a prayer
that forms you in the school of the living Gospel
educates your soul to piety,
makes you persevere in the good,
prepares you for life, and,
above all,
makes you dear to Most Holy Mary,
who will protect you
and defend you from evil.

Pray to Our Lady for me, too,
while I entrust each of you
to her maternal protection.

MARCH 3, 1984

From
The Loving Heart

Message for the First World Day of the Sick, 1993

Love for those who suffer is the sign and measure of the degree of civilization and progress of a people.

The Christian community has always paid special attention to the sick and to the world of suffering in its many manifestations. In the wake of that long tradition, the universal Church, with a renewed spirit of service, is preparing to celebrate the first World Day of the Sick as a special occasion for growth, with an attitude of *listening, reflection,* and *effective commitment* in the face of the great mystery of pain and illness. That Day, which beginning in February 1993 will be celebrated every year on February 11, the day of commemoration of Our Lady of Lourdes, seeks to be for all believers "a special time of prayer and sharing, of offering one's suffering for the good of the Church and of reminding everyone to see in his sick brother or sister the face of Christ, who, by suffering, dying, and rising, achieved the salvation of mankind."

The day seeks, further, to involve all people of goodwill. Indeed, the basic questions posed by the reality of suffering and the appeal to bring both physical and spiritual relief do not concern only believers but challenge all humanity, marked by the limitations of the mortal condition.

Unfortunately, we are preparing to celebrate this first World Day in circumstances that are dramatic for several reasons: the events of these months, while bringing out the urgency of prayer in asking for help from on High, recall us to the duty of launching new and urgent initiatives of help for those who suffer and cannot wait.

Before the eyes of all are the sad images of individuals and whole peoples who, lacerated by war and conflicts, succumb under the weight of easily avoidable calamities. How can we turn our gaze from the imploring faces of so many human beings, especially children, reduced to a shell of their former selves by hardships of every kind in which they are caught up against their will because of selfishness and violence? And how can we forget all those who at health-care facilities—hospitals, clinics, leprosariums, centers for the disabled, nursing homes—or in their own dwellings undergo the calvary of sufferings that are often neglected, not always suitably relieved, and sometimes even made worse by a lack of adequate support?

Illness, which in everyday experience is perceived as a frustration of the natural life force, for believers becomes an appeal to "read" the new, difficult situation *in the perspective that is proper to faith.* Outside of faith, moreover, how can we discover in the moment of trial the constructive contribution of pain? How can we give meaning and value to the anguish, unease, and physical and psychic ills accompanying our mortal condition? What justification can we find for the decline of old age and the final goal of death, which, in spite of all scientific and technological progress, inexorably remain?

Yes, *only in Christ,* the incarnate Word, Redeemer of mankind and victor over death, *is it possible to find satisfactory answers to such fundamental questions.*

In the light of Christ's death and Resurrection, illness no longer appears as an exclusively negative event; rather, it is seen as a "visit by God," an opportunity "to release love, in order to give birth to works of love toward our neighbor, in order to transform the whole of human civilization into a civilization of love."

The history of the Church and of Christian spirituality offers very broad testimony of this. Over the centuries shining pages have been written of heroism in suffering accepted and offered in union with Christ. And pages no less marvellous have been traced out through humble service to the poor and the sick, in whose tormented flesh the presence of the poor, crucified Christ has been recognized.

The celebration of the World Day of the Sick—in its preparation, its unfolding, and its objectives — is not meant to be reduced to a mere external display centering on certain initiatives, however praiseworthy they may be, but is intended to reach consciences to make them aware of the valuable contribution that human and Christian service to those suffering makes to better understanding among people and, consequently, to building real peace.

Indeed, peace presupposes, as its preliminary condition, that special attention be reserved for the suffering and the sick by public authorities, national and international organizations, and every person of goodwill. This is valid, first of all, for developing countries — in Latin America, Africa, and Asia — which are marked by serious deficiencies in health care. With the celebration of the World Day of the Sick, the Church is promoting a renewed commitment to those populations, and seeking to wipe out the injustice existing today by devoting greater human, spiritual, and material resources to their needs.

In this regard, I wish to address a special appeal to civil authorities, to people of science, and to all those who work directly with the sick. May their service never become bureaucratic and impersonal! Particularly, may it be quite clear to all that the administration of public money imposes the serious duty of avoiding its waste and improper use so that available resources, administered wisely and equitably, will serve to insure prevention of disease and care during illness for all who need them.

The hopes that are so alive today for a humanization of medicine and health care require a more decisive response. To make health care more humane and adequate it is, however, essential to draw on a transcendent vision of man which stresses the value and sacredness of life in the sick person as the image and child of God. Illness and pain affect every human being: love for the suffering is the sign and measure of the degree of civilization and progress of a people.

To you, dear sick people all over the world, the main actors of this World Day, may this event bring the announcement of the living and comforting presence of the Lord. Your sufferings, accepted and borne with unshakable faith, when joined to those of Christ, take on extraordinary value for the life of the Church and the good of humanity.

For you, health-care workers called to the highest, most meritorious, and exemplary testimony of justice and love, may this day be a renewed spur to continue in your delicate service, with generous openness to the profound values of the person, to respect for human dignity, and to the defense of life, from its beginning to its natural close.

For you, Pastors of the Christian people, and to all the different members of the Church community, for volunteers, and particularly for those engaged in the health-care ministry, may this World Day of the Sick offer stimulus and encouragement to go forward with fresh dedication on the way of service to tried, suffering humanity.

On the commemoration of Our Lady of Lourdes, whose shrine at the foot of the Pyrenees has become a temple of human suffering, we approach—as she did on Calvary, where the cross of her Son rose up—the crosses of pain and solitude of so many brothers and sisters to bring them comfort, to share their suffering and present it to the Lord of life in spiritual communion with the whole Church.

May the Blessed Virgin, Health of the Sick and Mother of the Living, be our support and our hope and, through the celebration of the Day of the Sick, increase our sensitivity and dedication to those being tested, along with the trusting expectation of the luminous day of our salvation, when every tear will be dried forever. May it be granted to us to enjoy the first fruits of that day from now on in the superabundant joy—though in the midst of all tribulations—promised by Christ which no one can take from us.

My blessing on all!

FROM THE VATICAN, OCTOBER 21, 1992
MESSAGE FOR FEBRUARY 11, 1993,
FIRST WORLD DAY OF THE SICK

The sick,
the afflicted

It is these especially to whom,
at the very start of our pastoral ministry,
we wish to open our heart.
Is it not in fact you,
brothers and sisters,
who with your sufferings
share the passion of the Redeemer himself
and in some way complete it?
The unworthy successor of Peter,
who proposes to examine
the unfathomable riches of Christ,
sorely needs your help,
your prayer,
your sacrifice,
and for this reason
most humbly entreats you.

FIRST *URBI ET ORBI* MESSAGE,
OCTOBER 17, 1978

The incomparable effectiveness of suffering

Today I would like to address all sick people in a special way, as one who, like them, is ill, and offer a word of comfort and hope.

When, the day after my election to the throne of Peter, I visited the Gemelli Hospital, I said that I wished "to support my papal ministry above all on those who suffer."

Providence arranged that I should return to the Gemelli Hospital as a sick person myself. I will now reiterate the same conviction I held then: suffering, accepted in union with Christ who suffers, has an incomparable effectiveness in the realization of the divine plan of salvation. And here I will say again with St. Paul: "Now I rejoice in my sufferings for your sake, and in my flesh I complete what is lacking in Christ's afflictions for the sake of his body, that is, the Church."

I invite all sick people to join with me in offering their sufferings to Christ for the good of the Church and mankind. May Most Holy Mary sustain and comfort us.

AT THE GEMELLI HOSPITAL,
AFTER THE ASSASSINATION ATTEMPT,
MAY 24, 1981

With me, offer your ordeal to the Lord

Dear ones, you who are sick, handicapped, or in frail health, and who are present at the Eucharistic Congress,

My affectionate thoughts and my prayers go out to all who have gathered at the grotto of Lourdes, but to you in a very special way.

Lourdes is the place where the sick, who come from all over the world, are always first, helped by their healthy brothers and sisters to offer their sufferings to the compassion of our Mother, the Virgin Mary, and to the mercy of Jesus Christ, and to leave with the comfort that comes from God.

You are closest to the heart of this Congress, which celebrates the real presence of Christ in the humble spoil of bread, the Christ who suffered and offered his Passion so that we might enter into Life and his Kingdom be opened to us.

You do not cease at any moment to be full members of the Church; not only, like others, are you in communion with the Body of the Lord, but in your flesh you are in communion with the Passion of Christ. Your sufferings are not in vain: they contribute, invisibly, to the growth in Charity that animates the Church. The sacrament of Anointing of the Sick joins you in a special way to Christ, for the forgiveness of your sins, for the comfort of your body and soul, for the increasing hope of the Kingdom of Light and Life that Christ promises you.

Whenever I meet with the sick, in Rome or during my travels, I stop with each of them, I listen to them, I bless them, just as Jesus did, to show that each one is the object of God's tenderness.

At this moment God has allowed me to endure, in my own flesh, suffering and weakness. This makes me feel even closer to you, it helps me understand your ordeal even better. "Now I rejoice in my sufferings for your sake, and in my flesh I complete what is lacking in Christ's afflictions for the sake of his body, that is, the Church." I invite you to offer, together with me, your suffering to the Lord, who, through the Cross, achieves great things; to offer it so that the entire Church, through the Eucharist, may undergo a renewal of faith and charity; so that the world may know the benefit of forgiveness, of peace, of love.

May Our Lady of Lourdes sustain you in hope!

I bless all those who help you with their friendship and their care and who receive spiritual support from you.

And I bless you yourselves with all my affection, in the name of the Father and the Son and the Holy Spirit.

MESSAGE TO THE SICK
ASSEMBLED AT THE GROTTO OF LOURDES,
JULY 21, 1981

The "community" of the sick

Grateful as I am for the gift of life saved and health restored, I would like to express my gratitude for something more: that I have been granted the privilege, during these three months, to belong, dear brothers and sisters, to your community: to the community of the sick who are suffering in this hospital, and who for that reason constitute a special organism in the Church: in the mystical body of Christ. In a special way, according to St. Paul, one can say of them that they complete what is lacking in Christ's afflictions for the sake of his body. During these months I have had the privilege of belonging to this particular organism. And for that, too, I kindly thank you, brothers and sisters, at this moment, as I take my leave of you and your community.

Certainly there were and are among you many whose sufferings, incomparably greater than mine, and endured with love, bring you much closer to the Crucifixion and the Redeemer.

I have thought of this more than once, and so, as your Bishop, I have embraced all of you in my prayers. And sometimes I receive news of those whom the Lord of life has called to himself during these months.

All this, dear brothers and sisters, I have experienced daily, and I would like to tell you about it today, as I bid you farewell. Now I know better than ever before that *suffering* is one of those dimensions of life in which more than ever *the grace of redemption is grafted onto the human heart.* And if I wish that each and every one of you may regain your health and leave this hospital, then with equal warmth I hope that you may take away from there the profound graft of divine life, which the grace of suffering carries with it.

AUGUST 14, 1981

Suffering asks us to be like Christ

I, too, have been assailed by suffering and have known the physical weakness that comes from disability and illness.

It is precisely because I have experienced suffering that I am able to repeat the words of St. Paul with even greater conviction: "Neither death, nor life, nor angels, nor principalities, nor things present, nor things to come, nor powers, nor height, nor depth, nor anything else in all creation, will be able to separate us from the love of God in Christ Jesus our Lord."

Dear friends, no force or power exists that can separate you from God's love. Illness and suffering seem contradictory to what is important for man and what man desires. And yet no malady, no weakness, no infirmity can deprive you of your dignity as children of God, as brothers and sisters of Jesus Christ.

By dying on the cross, Christ reveals to us the meaning of our suffering. In his Passion we find the encouragement and strength to avoid every temptation to bitterness and, through pain, to grow into a new life. *Suffering is an invitation to be like the Son by doing the will of the Father.* We are offered the opportunity to imitate Christ, who died to redeem mankind from sin. Thus the Father wished suffering to enrich the individual and the whole Church.

UNITED KINGDOM, MAY 28, 1982

I entrust to the Lord the sufferings of all sick people

Dearest brothers and sisters,

Today I am reciting the Angelus in a hospital, a place of suffering and hope, together with the doctors and the patients.

The expressions of solidarity that have come from all over the world have been a comfort to me.

Thank you! Thanks to the doctors and staff members of the Gemelli Hospital and the Vatican, who have been so attentive and so solicitous of me; thanks to those who in various ways have expressed their spiritual closeness with affectionate good wishes; thanks above all for the prayers, the most pleasing gift and the most effective means for getting through the harsh and painful moments of existence with faith and serenity.

Dearest brothers and sisters, I greet you and bless you all.

With the recitation of the Angelus, I entrust to the Lord, through the hands of Mary, the physical and spiritual sufferings of all the sick people in the world, together with my own, for the Church and for mankind.

RECITATION OF THE ANGELUS AT THE GEMELLI HOSPITAL,
JULY 19, 1992

Meeting with the old, the sick, and the handicapped always has a privileged place during my pastoral visits. You are not the forgotten children of God. On the contrary! Just as a sick child has a special place in the heart of its parents, so is God's joy in your faith and your courage that much greater. And Jesus Christ has assured us that it is in you that we meet him in a special way.

Unfortunately in the world of today not everyone realizes that those who are afflicted with old age, sickness, or a handicap have the same value as other human beings. And yet God is not interested in how productive we are or in the size of our bank account. The Lord looks not at appearances but at the heart.

God's loving gaze as it rests on each man and woman gives us the assurance that—old or young, healthy or sick—we are wanted or wished for, without exception. For this reason we all feel that we are sons and daughters of the same heavenly Father. God's love for us comes first and is fundamental. To experience this and to be conscious of it is truly something great; and it is important to participate in this experience with others and share it with them in life.

AUSTRIA, JUNE 26, 1988

When people meet for the first time and wish to become friends, they usually introduce themselves. Do we need to do that? You already know my name and a lot about me. But, since I intend to become friends with you, I want to introduce myself: I come to you as a missionary sent by the Father and by Jesus to proclaim the Kingdom of God that begins in this world but is realized only in eternity; to consolidate the faith of my brothers and sisters; and to create a profound communion among all the children of the same Church. I come as the minister and unworthy vicar of Christ to watch over his Church; as the humble successor to the Apostle Peter, the Bishop of Rome, and Pastor of the Universal Church.

Like Peter, I have agreed to be the universal Pastor of the Church, eager to know, love, and serve all the members of the flock entrusted to me. I am here to know you. My affection for all and each of you is vast. I am sure that in some way, at least, I will be able to serve you.

BRAZIL, LEPROSARIUM OF MARITUBA,
JULY 8, 1980

And you, who are you? For me you are first of all human beings, endowed with the immense dignity that is a condition of being a person, each one of you with the unique, unrepeatable personal features that God has given you. You are persons who have been saved by the blood of the One whom I like to call the "Redeemer of man," as I did in the first letter I wrote to the entire Church and the world. You are children of God, known and loved by him. You are and will be from now on and forever my friends, my very dear friends.

Therefore, blessed is God who grants us the grace of this meeting. It is indeed a grace for me, like the Lord Jesus whose minister and representative I am, to meet the poor and the sick, for whom He had a real preference. It is true that I cannot, like him, cure the ills of the body, but he will give me, through his goodness, the capacity to bring some comfort to hearts and souls. In this sense I hope that our meeting will be a grace for you, too. It is in the name of Jesus that we are here assembled: may he be among us as he promised.

BRAZIL, LEPROSARIUM OF MARITUBA,
JULY 8, 1980

God wants to be close to every human being, but he is close to the sick with particular tenderness.

Yet human suffering leads us to doubt the words of Jesus that the Kingdom of God is near. When pain obscures the mind and weakens the body and soul, God may seem very far away, and life can become an intolerable burden. We are tempted not to believe in the Good News. Because, as the Book of Wisdom says, "A perishable body weighs down the soul, and this earthly tent burdens the thoughtful mind." The mystery of human suffering oppresses the sick person, and new and anxious questions arise:

Why does God let me suffer?
To what purpose?
How can God, who is so good,
    allow so much evil?

There are no easy answers for the questions posed by the minds and hearts of the afflicted. But we cannot find a satisfactory response without the light of faith. We must call to God, our Father and Creator, as the author of the Book of Wisdom did:

"With thee is wisdom, who knows they works . . .
Send her forth from the holy heavens . . .
that she may be with me and toil, and
that I may learn what is pleasing to thee."

NEW ZEALAND, NOVEMBER 23, 1986

217

"Lord, tell me the truth on your Cross"

In the eyes of the world, suffering, illness, and death are frightening, futile, and destructive. Especially when children have to suffer, when human beings who are innocent — and they are the majority — are stricken by illness, a handicap, or incurable pain, we find ourselves before an *enigma*, which we cannot honestly resolve by human means alone. It can make us cruel, it can embitter not only the one who is directly affected but also those who are close to him, and who, powerless to bring aid, suffer on account of that powerlessness.

Why? Why me? Why now? Why my wife, my father, my sister, my friend? These questions are understandable. On this earth no one can answer that "why." And yet the question "to what purpose" has this burden been placed on me can open up new horizons to us. When Jesus was asked if it was the blind man who sinned or his parents, he answered against every expectation: "It was not that this man sinned, or his parents, but that the works of God might be made manifest in him."

With this premise, the question "to what purpose" suggests an even more important word, which can provide the determining direction: "To what purpose, Lord?" This is no longer an insignificant question, which falls into the void, but, rather, is addressed to one who has suffered and has struggled to the last drop of blood, who "with loud cries and tears," as one reads in the Letter to the Hebrews, "learned obedience." He understands you and knows how you feel; he himself, at an early moment, prayed that the bitter cup be taken away. But he was so obedient to the will of the Father that in the end he could give his total and free assent. *From him you can learn to make your suffering rich in fruits and in meaning for the salvation of the world.* With him your illness and suffering can make you better men, and even happier and freer. Many have learned from him and so have been changed, by the source of comfort. Therefore go to the school of his suffering for our salvation and repeat the prayer that St. Catherine of Siena addressed to Christ during her many trials: "Lord, tell me the truth on your Cross, I want to listen to you."

As Christians, we see in illness not a grim or even senseless human destiny but, in the end, the mystery of the Cross and of the resurrection of Christ. In pain and suffering man shares the fate of creation, which — as St. Paul says — through sin has been "subjected to futility," which "has been groaning in travail," but which at the same time has already been animated by the hope that it "will be set free from its bondage to decay and obtain the glorious liberty of the children of God."

For a believer, illness and suffering are not a tragic fate that must be passively endured but, rather, a task, thanks to which he can live his Christian vocation in a special way. They are *the invocation of God to mankind:* an invocation to us to be fraternally close to those who are suffering and to help them using all the means offered by medical science; an invocation to the sick not to resign themselves to their suffering, or rebel out of bitterness, but, rather, to recognize in it *the possibility of a more intense form of following Christ.* Faith alone can give us courage and strength. If we are trustfully accepting, every human suffering can become personal participation in the offering of Christ who suffered for our sins in order to save the world. Thus the Passion of Christ continues in the individual who suffers. So, too, all the help and love we can manifest are in the end addressed to Christ. "I was sick and you visited me," Christ says, and continues, "Truly, I say to you, as you did it to one of the least of these my brethren, you did it to me."

Through the inner communion of suffering with Christ, human suffering receives a liberating and transforming power and by the same means *participates in the paschal hope* of future resurrection.

SWITZERLAND, JUNE 16, 1984

219

Give me your sufferings,
Brothers and sisters!
I will bring them to the altar,
to offer them to God the Father,
in communion with those
of his only begotten Son
and to pray,
in their name,
for peace for the Church,
mutual understanding among nations,
the humility of repentance for those who have sinned,
the generosity of forgiveness
for those who have been injured —
for all the joy
of a renewed experience
of the merciful love of God.
May the Most Holy Virgin,
who was "standing by the Cross of Jesus"
when he died for us,
rouse in our hearts
feelings suitable
for this hour of light and grace.
Amen.

SANCTUARY OF COLLEVALENZA,
NOVEMBER 22, 1981

To the victims of AIDS

I address myself above all, with heartfelt solicitude, *to those who are afflicted with AIDS.*

Brothers in Christ, who know all the bitterness of the way of the Cross, be assured that you are not alone. *The Church* is with you, with the sacrament of salvation, to sustain you on your difficult road. The Church receives a great deal from your suffering, if it is confronted in faith; the Church is beside you with the comfort of the active solidarity of its members, so that you will never lose hope. Do not forget the call of Jesus: "Come unto me, who labor and are heavy laden, and I will give you rest."

With you, dearest ones, are *men of science,* who work tirelessly to contain and defeat this grave illness; with you are many who, as health professionals or as volunteers, sustained by the ideal of human solidarity, will attend to you with devoted care and every means available.

You, in turn, can offer something significant to the community that you belong to. The effort that you make to give meaning to your suffering is a precious reminder to all of the highest values of life and a perhaps decisive support for those who are tempted by desperation. Do not be shut up in yourselves, but try and accept the help of your brothers and sisters.

The Church raises up prayers to the Lord for you every day, and especially for those of you who suffer your illness in abandonment, in solitude; for orphans, for the weakest, for the poorest, whom the Lord has taught us to consider the first in his kingdom.

AT THE INTERNATIONAL CONGRESS ON AIDS,
NOVEMBER 15, 1989

Sooner or later
sorrow knocks at our door
and, even if we don't want to open to it,
it enters tragically into our existence.
Christian faith
tells us not to lose heart,
but to maintain a deep and living hope,
to trust in God
who neither abandons nor forgets,
to look at Jesus crucified,
the divine Word incarnate
who wanted to suffer like us and for us.
Then the desire,
which cannot be realized,
becomes a hope for quick and complete healing.
All of us know in fact
how precious health is, which enables us to work,
to be interested in various activities,
to pledge ourselves to the needs
of the family and society,
to bring our concrete
and effective contribution
to the development and progress of society.

MARCH 23, 1985

Suffering is a mysterious call

Suffering is a vocation to love more: it is a mysterious call to share in the infinite love of God for mankind, that love which led God to become flesh and to die nailed to the Cross!

The society we live in is tormented by so many problems: the multitude of ideologies, the variety of anthropologies, the complexity of social and political events, the fragmentary nature of personal experiences, the tendency to selfishness, the spread of permissiveness, and, at the same time, anxiety, dissatisfaction, and fear of the future have created a situation so complicated and difficult that we increasingly feel a need to believe the enlightening and saving message of Christ, to love in his name, and to invoke the mercy of the Almighty. The times urge us to accept our cross with courage and serenity, in order to bear witness to the presence of God in human history, revive the meaning of eternity, and instill hope and trust.

"Grant, O my God! that I may adore in silence the order of thy adorable providence in the direction of my life": so said Pascal in the famous Prayer to Ask of God the Proper Use of Sickness. And asking the Lord for his divine consolations, he added: "Grant, my God, that in a constantly equal uniformity of spirit I may receive all kinds of events . . . that such as I am, I may conform myself to thy will; and that being sick as I am, I may glorify thee in my sufferings."

Especially today, in modern society, we can see the immense value of Christian suffering, and every local community must carry out the "pastoral of suffering," fully incorporating the sick and suffering into the various apostolic initiatives and activities.

MAY 23, 1987

The "word of the Cross" has a message for you health-care workers, who, at various levels and with varying responsibilities, do your jobs in hospitals.

It is Jesus Christ who hides and is revealed in the face and in the flesh, in the heart and in the soul of those whom you are called to help and to care for. He considers done to himself what is done to the least of these brothers, who are ill and often alone and marginalized by society.

This requires of you words, gestures, and inner attitudes inspired not only by a profound and rich humanity but by a genuine spirit of faith and charity.

I therefore ask you, and through you, all those who work in health-care facilities, to overcome the temptation to indifference and selfishness and to do your utmost above all *to humanize these health-care environments and make them more livable,* in such a way that the sick may be cured in the totality of their body and soul. Do your utmost so that all the *fundamental rights and values of the human being* may be recognized and supported, and above all the right to life, from its beginning to its natural end. That requires attention to different situations, respectful and patient dialogue, generous love for every man and woman considered as the image of God and, for those who are believers, an "icon" of Christ who suffers.

APRIL 1, 1990

I wish to express to the doctors, nurses, and health-care aides my deep appreciation and respect for the skill and attention they bring to the practice of their professions. This is a true vocation, undertaken for the care of our brothers and sisters who suffer. Few other professions are so worthy and honorable as that of the doctor who works with commitment and has strong ethical and humanitarian feelings. It approaches a sort of priesthood whose mission consists in healing the body and also in comforting the soul.

Thus I urge these professionals to be aware of the value of their mission, always to serve life and never death, to be completely honest in the choice of treatments and surgical interventions, not to yield to the temptation for money, not to abandon their country for purely material gains, and to see in their patients—even the poorest, who at times cannot pay for their services—human beings and children of God.

I commend to the Lord all those who work on behalf of the sick in hospitals, clinics, and hospices. I wish to repeat to all, doctors, nurses, chaplains, and hospital personnel: yours is a noble vocation. Remember that you serve Christ in the sufferings of your brothers and sisters.

BOLIVIA, MAY 12, 1988

Make medicine more humane

Since it is part of the tradition of the Church to consider Christian everything that is authentically human, I feel it is my duty to call on you urgently to make your practice of medicine more humane, and to establish a frank bond of solidarity with your patients, one that goes beyond a professional relationship. The sick person secretly expects this from you. Besides, he stands before you in all his nobility as a human being who, in spite of being needy, suffering, and perhaps even crippled, should not for that reason be considered a passive object. On the contrary, a person is always a subject and should be approached as such. This is the inborn dignity of man. A person by his nature needs a personal relationship. Even someone who is sick is never just a clinical case but always a "sick *person*"; he expects competent and effective care from you, but he also expects the capacity and skill to inspire trust, even to the point where you can discuss the situation honestly with him and, above all, display a sincere attitude of "sym-pathy" (feeling with), in the etymological sense of the word, so as to translate into practice the words of the Apostle Paul, which echoed those of an ancient wise man: "Rejoice with those who are happy, weep with those who are in pain."

AT A MEDICAL CONVENTION
ON THE TREATMENT OF TUMORS,
FEBRUARY 25, 1982

Make medicine and hospitals more humane

In every part of the world we see vigorous growth in the phenomenon of the volunteer, with a great number of persons, especially among the young, offering to spend at least part of their time working, without pay, on behalf of the community. For Christians, to take on that responsibility for the common good is a practical way of demonstrating their willingness to follow the example of Christ by sharing the problems and difficulties of their brothers and sisters.

How can we fail to give proper thanks to the important contribution that the loving and modest presence of volunteers brings to the promise of healing and care, complementing the work of the nursing personnel?

Volunteer service, if properly coordinated, can help to improve the quality of care, adding an extra touch of human warmth and attention, which can obviously comfort the patient and perhaps even have a positive effect on the outcome of the treatment.

I know that in a considerable number of Catholic hospitals, especially in the wards for the chronically ill, much has been done in this field.

But the present circumstances would seem to suggest that it is time to make an attempt to broaden the use of the generous resources available in the community, and to this purpose it would be useful for hospitals run on a Christian basis to share their aspirations. The goal is a structure of health-care assistance that is not isolated but, rather, a vital part of the social fabric that surrounds it. An active exchange between the community of the healthy and the community of the sick will surely provide a powerful incentive for an increase in charity.

The Catholic hospitals are charged with great responsibilities at the moment, and their survival depends on the fact that Catholics occupy themselves not only with the sick but with all people. Their survival, similarly, depends on this: on whether Catholics can create a new culture and new forms of pastoral assistance for the sick, testifying to the fact that Christ is the savior of the soul as well as of the body.

To the health-care workers in Catholic hospitals,
October 31, 1985

I commend to you the Church and the world

As I walked down the nave of the Church, I shook hands with all those who were nearby. Then, through them, this gesture was transmitted to the others. This is a significant sign: I gave you my hands to demonstrate to you that we are joined, or, rather, to show you my deep desire to be more closely joined. I strongly wish for this union with the suffering; it is my strength, because my strength is the Cross of Christ, and the Cross of Christ is present in your suffering.

I wish to embrace all of you, and each one of you, and I would like to be close to each of you. I commend myself to your prayers and your sacrifices. I commend myself, and I commend the whole Church and the world, a world that runs a greater and greater risk, and has always a greater need for the Cross and for redemption. This is why I commend to you the Church and the world, and also my person, the person of the Pope who must serve the Church and the world.

RIMINI, AUGUST 29, 1982

Sick people and the Rosary

I heartily urge you, sick people and all the rest of you, friends, relatives, priests, and religious, to pray to Our Lady every day with the Holy Rosary.

Since health is a good that is part of the original plan of creation, to recite the rosary for sick people, so that they may be cured or at least obtain relief from their suffering, is an exquisitely Christian and human service; it is always consoling and always effective, because it instills serenity and strength of spirit. And when the illness persists and suffering remains, the Rosary also reminds us that the redemption of mankind is brought about by means of the Cross. Meditation on the mysteries of salvation, which has been obtained for us on the Cross of the Redeemer, who became flesh for love of us, gives us a fundamental understanding of the value of suffering for the Church, for the return to grace of those who live in error and sin, and for the conversion of those who are alienated from God, from Christ, or from the Church. The silent, hidden suffering of a sick person is worth more than all the clamor of many discussions and arguments. "A spark of pure love," St. John of the Cross wrote, "is more precious in the eyes of God and in those of the soul than any other thing; love is the purpose for which we were created. Without prayer and without union with God, everything is reduced to a pointless hammering, and we seem to be doing little more than nothing, and sometimes in fact nothing, indeed, often we may even be doing harm." We read, in the biography of St. Bernadette, that when she recited the Rosary she emphasized in particular the words "Pray for us sinners." To anyone who noticed this, she responded: "Oh, yes! We must pray for sinners. The Holy Virgin urges it. We can never do enough for the conversion of sinners." Since she was almost always ill, Bernadette said: "My task is to be sick: to suffer is my duty. Prayer is my only weapon: I cannot do other than pray and suffer!"

And this is also the message left at Fatima by Our Lady to the three children: suffering and the Rosary for the Church and for sinners.

The people who care for the sick may draw from the Rosary the strength to be always kind, loving, and patient toward those who suffer, and respectful of their pain.

ORISTANO, OCTOBER 18, 1985

For my part, I rely on you: as I ask for the help of the prayers of the monks and the nuns and many other holy persons that the Spirit may inspire and give strength to my pontifical ministry, so I ask the precious help that can come to me from the offering of your sufferings and your illness. May this offering be joined to your prayers; or, rather, transformed into prayers for me, for my immediate coworkers, and for all those who entrust to me their afflictions and their sorrows, their needs and their wants.

But why not begin this prayer immediately?

Lord,
with the faith that you have given us,
we confess to you, omnipotent God,
our Creator and provident Father,
God of hope
in Jesus Christ our Savior,
God of love,
in the Holy Spirit, our Consoler!

Lord,
trusting in your promises
that are eternal,
we wish to come to you always,
to find in you
relief from our suffering.

Yet, being disciples of Jesus,
we cannot do as we wish,
but do your will
in all our living!

Lord,
grateful for the love
of Christ

for the lepers who have had
the good fortune to come in contact with Him,
we see ourselves in them . . .
we thank you also for the encouragement
we receive in everything that helps us,
brings us relief, and comforts us:
we thank you
for the medicine and the doctors,
for the care and the nurses,
for our living conditions,
for those who comfort us
and who are by us comforted,
for those who understand us
and accept us for the others.

Lord,
grant us patience, serenity, and courage;
allow us to live a joyful charity,
for your love,
toward those who suffer more than we do
and toward those who, not suffering,
do not have a clear sense of the meaning of life.

Lord,
we want our life to be useful,
we wish to serve:
to praise, thank,
shelter, and pray, with Christ,
for those who adore you
and for those who do not adore you,
in the world, and for your Church,
scattered throughout the earth.

Lord,
through the infinite merits of Christ

on the Cross, your "suffering servant"
and our brother, with whom we are joined,
we pray to you for our families,
friends, and benefactors,
and for good results from the Pope's visit
and for Brazil. So let it be.

BRAZIL, JULY 8, 1980

You, too, dearest sick people, place yourselves under the Blessed Virgin's protective mantle, and you, too, ask her for comfort. And you are right to do so. Aren't the horsemen of the Apocalypse forever on the road, under forever new names? Even if we have never experienced pestilence, or plague, there are many other illnesses and ordeals that afflict men today. Despite all the progress of medicine, incurable diseases still exist, and often cause overwhelming anguish. And doesn't the scourge of war, which has struck us so many times, loom over the world today, with the threat of millions dead and unimaginable destruction? And who is not familiar with the terrifying images of hunger that we see every day in so many regions of the earth? In all these situations of hardship and suffering, and in so many others that I cannot enumerate here, we as believers must seek refuge in Mary, just as our fathers before us did. Yes, my dear ones, let us pray always and at all times: Holy Mary Mother of God, pray for us. That does not mean averting our gaze from problems, nor is it a matter of fleeing in the face of need or danger; it is simply Christian trust in the help of God, who gave us Mary as our mother. And does a mother exist whose children cannot ask her for help?

LUXEMBOURG, MAY 15, 1985

235

We look at Mary just as Elizabeth did, seeing her arrive with a hurried step and hearing her voice in greeting: "As soon as the sound of your greeting reached my ears, the baby in my womb leaped for joy."

How can we not meditate on this first call to reflection? Elizabeth's leap for joy points out the gift that can be contained in a simple greeting, when it comes from a heart overflowing with God. How often can the darkness of solitude, which oppresses a soul, be pierced by the luminous ray of a smile and a kind word!

A kind word is quickly said; and yet at times it is difficult for us to utter it. Weariness deters us, anxiety constricts us, a feeling of coldness or of selfish indifference restrains us. Thus it happens that we pass by even people we know without looking them in the face and without realizing how often they are suffering from that subtle, debilitating pain that comes from feeling ignored. A cordial word would be enough, an affectionate gesture, and immediately something would reawaken in them: a nod of attention and politeness can be a gust of fresh air in the mustiness of an existence that is oppressed by sadness and discouragement. Mary's greeting filled her old cousin Elizabeth's heart with joy.

FEBRUARY 11, 1981

The message of Lourdes

At Lourdes Mary reminded the world that the meaning of life on earth is its orientation toward Heaven.

Our Lady, at Lourdes, came to speak to man of "paradise," so that although he was actively engaged in the building of a more welcoming and a more just world, he would not forget to lift his eyes to Heaven to draw from it guidance and hope.

The Most Holy Virgin came, furthermore, to remind us of the value of conversion and penance, again presenting to the world the heart of the evangelical message. She said to Bernadette,* during the appearance of February 18: "I promise to make you happy not in this world but in the next." Later, she asked her to pray for the conversion of sinners and on February 24 she repeated three times: "Penance, penance, penance!"

At Lourdes, Mary emphatically points out the reality of the Redemption of mankind from sin through the Cross, which is to say through suffering. God himself, having become man, wished to die innocent, nailed to a cross!

At Lourdes, Our Lady teaches the redemptive value of suffering; it bestows courage, patience, resignation; it illuminates the mystery of our participation in the passion of Christ; it raises our inner gaze to true and complete happiness, which Jesus himself has assured and prepared for us beyond life and history. Bernadette had understood Mary's message perfectly, and had become a nun in Nevers. She was gravely ill, but when anyone entreated her to go to the grotto of Massabielle to pray for a cure she answered: "Lourdes is not for me!" She was subject to powerful asthmatic attacks, and

---

* St. Bernadette, Bernadette Soubirous (1844–79), saw a vision of the Virgin Mary in a cave near Lourdes in 1858. At the site, Bernadette discovered a spring with healing powers. A chapel was built at the cave, the Grotto of Massabielle, and millions of pilgrims visit Lourdes each year. Bernadette Soubirous was canonized by Pope Pius XI in 1933. Her body has lain in a shrine at the Chapel of the Convent of St. Gildard at Nevers since 1925.

when a novice nurse asked her, "Do you suffer a lot?" she answered simply: "It is necessary!" Ultimately, the message of Lourdes is completed by the invitation to prayer: Mary appears in the attitude of praying, asks Bernadette to recite the Rosary with her own personal crown, asks her to build a chapel there, and to have people come in procession.

This, too, is an admonition that is still valid. Our Lady of Lourdes came to tell us, with the authority and kindness of a Mother, that if we truly want to sustain, strengthen, and spread the Christian faith, humble, trustful prayer is needed.

FEBRUARY 11, 1987

Faith alleviates suffering

At Lourdes, Mary undertakes as her mission the relief of suffering and the reconciliation of our souls with God and our neighbor.

The graces that this Mother of mercy obtains for the immense crowds of suffering, lost humanity all have the purpose of leading men and women to Christ and obtaining for them the gift of his Spirit.

At Lourdes Mary, through St. Bernadette, revealed herself conspicuously as "the voice of the will of the Son."

Everything that Our Lady said to the Seer, everything that she urged her to do, everything that began at Lourdes, that happened and is happening there, reflects, if you wish, the "will" of Our Lady: but in Whose name has She obtained all this, in Whose grace, if not that of her divine Son?

So we can say that Lourdes belongs to Christ even more than to his Most Holy Mother.

At Lourdes we learn to know Christ through Mary. The miracles of Lourdes and the miracles of Christ, achieved through the intercession of Mary.

For this reason Lourdes is an honored place of Christian *experience*.

At Lourdes we learn to suffer as Christ suffered. We accept suffering as he accepted it.

At Lourdes our suffering is alleviated because it is lived with Christ. *Provided* one lives it with Christ, supported by Mary.

At Lourdes we learn that faith does not alleviate suffering in the sense of lessening it physically. This is the task of medicine, or, very rarely, it may happen miraculously.

At Lourdes we learn that faith alleviates suffering by making it acceptable as a means of expiation and as an expression of love.

At Lourdes we learn to offer ourselves not only to divine justice but also — as St. Theresa of Lisieux* put it — to the merciful love of the one who, as I said in my Apostolic Letter *Salvifici Doloris,* suffered "voluntarily and innocently."

The Christian, like every other person of feeling and conscience, has a duty to work generously to bring about the alleviation of suffering, in order to obtain health — for himself or for others.

But his principal concern is to eliminate the most profound evil, sin. Vigorous physical health would be worthless if the soul were not at peace with God. If, however, the soul is in God's grace, even the most terrific pain will be made bearable, because the soul will understand its value for eternal health, our own and that of our brothers and sisters.

FEBRUARY II, 1988

---

* St. Theresa of Lisieux (1873–97) was a Carmelite nun who wrote about her short life in *The Story of a Soul.* Known as the Little Flower of Jesus, Thérèse Martin was canonized by Pope Pius XI in 1925 and was made a Doctor of the Church by John Paul II in 1997, only the third woman to be accorded this honor.

Why is it the sick who make pilgrimages to Lourdes? Why—we ask ourselves—has that place become for them a sort of "Cana in Galilee," to which they feel drawn in a special way? What attracts them to Lourdes with such force?

These people, if they are inspired by faith, turn to Lourdes. Why? Because they know that, as at Cana, "Jesus' Mother is there": and where she is so, too, is her Son. This is the certainty that drives the multitudes who every year pour into Lourdes in search of relief, of comfort, of hope. Sick people of every kind make the pilgrimage to Lourdes, sustained by the hope that, through Mary, the saving power of Christ may be manifested. And, in fact, that power is always revealed, by the gift of immense serenity and resignation; in some cases there is a general improvement in health, or even the grace of a complete cure, as numerous "instances" attest, which have been verified in the course of more than a hundred years.

However, the miraculous cure, in spite of everything, remains an exceptional event.

The saving power of Christ propitiated by the intercession of his mother is revealed at Lourdes *in the spiritual dimension above all.* It is in the hearts of the sick that Mary allows the thaumaturgical voice of her Son to be heard: a voice that generously melts the harsh iron core of bitterness and rebelliousness, and gives the soul eyes with which to see in a new light the world, and others, and our own destiny.

The sick discover at Lourdes the value of their own suffering. In the light of faith they are able to understand the fundamental meaning that suffering can have not only in their own life, inwardly renewed by that flame which consumes and transforms, but also in the life of the Church, the mystical body of Christ.

The Most Holy Virgin, who, standing courageously beside the Cross of her son on Calvary, shared in his Passion herself, can always persuade new souls to unite their sufferings to the sacrifice of Christ, in a choral "offering" that, bridging time and space, embraces all mankind and saves it.

FEBRUARY 11, 1980

With its participation in suffering the Church becomes the dwelling place of God

Dear brothers and sisters! Of course there are always people who will carelessly and indifferently pass by you. They will make you feel insignificant and useless. But you may be sure that *we need you!* All society needs you. You continually question your neighbors about the profound meaning of human existence. You stimulate their solidarity, test their capacity to love. Above all, you challenge young people to give the best of themselves.

You inspire them to solidarity and willingness to help those who have a greater need for help. Where this solidarity is stifled, society is deprived of human warmth. Yet it is encouraging to see that many young people today are committed to serving the old, the sick, and the handicapped.

While I am with you, I wish to address all society: there should be no discrimination with regard to the value of human life. This discrimination gave rise, some decades ago, to one of the worst barbarities. There are not some lives that have value and others that do not. Every human life both before and after birth, whether it has fulfilled its potential or is handicapped — every human life has received its dignity from God, and no one can violate it. Every man is made in the image of God!

In conclusion I wish to repeat again that the Church needs you. *In you we recognize the presence of Christ who continues to live among us marked by the cross and by suffering.* And if you accept the sufferings that are inflicted on you, your prayer and your sacrifice to God will have an incredible force. Therefore pray at all times!

Pray and sacrifice for the Church and for the salvation of men, and also pray for my apostolic mission.

AUSTRIA, JUNE 26, 1988

242

Arise

How many times and on how many occasions do men need this invitation repeated to them?

ARISE

You who are disappointed,

ARISE

You who have no more hope,

ARISE

You who are used to misery and no longer believe that one can build something new.

ARISE

because God is about to make "all things new."

ARISE

You who are inured to God's gifts

ARISE

You who have lost the capacity to wonder

ARISE

You who have lost the confidence to call God "father"

ARISE

and regain your admiration for God's goodness.

ARISE

You who suffer

ARISE

You to whom life seems to have denied much

ARISE

while you feel excluded, abandoned, marginalized:

ARISE

because Christ has shown you his love and reserves for you an unhoped-for possibility of fulfillment.

ARISE

JUNE 8, 1986

Epilogue

Hora Tertia for the One-Month Memorial
of the Terrorist Attacks of September 11, 2001

Brothers and Sisters,
Dear Synodal Fathers,
one month since the inhumane terrorist attacks
which occurred in different parts of the United States of America,
we again commend
to the eternal mercy of the God of our Fathers
the numerous innocent victims.

We ask for consolation and comfort
for their family and relatives,
burdened by pain;
we invoke strength and courage
for the many who continue their work
in the places struck by this terrible disaster;
we implore tenacity and perseverance
by all men of goodwill
continuing on the paths of justice and peace.

May the Lord remove from the heart of man
every trace of resentment, of hostility and of hate,
and open him to reconciliation,
to solidarity and to peace.

Let us pray so that the "culture of love"
may be established all over the world.

After reciting the Our Father and
before the Apostolic Benediction,
the Holy Father pronounced the following prayer:

O God, Almighty and Merciful,
he who sows discord cannot understand you,
he who loves violence cannot welcome you:
watch over us in our painful human condition
tried by the brutal acts of terrorism and death;
Comfort your children and open our hearts to hope,
that our time may again know days of serenity and peace.
Through Christ our Lord.

OCTOBER 11, 2001

From Urbi et Orbi *message, Christmas 2002*

Christmas is a mystery of peace!
From the cave of Bethlehem
there rises today an urgent appeal
to the world not to yield
to mistrust, suspicion, and discouragement,
even though the tragic reality of terrorism
feeds uncertainties and fears.
Believers of all religions,
together with men and women of goodwill,
by outlawing all forms of intolerance and discrimination,
are called to build peace:
in *the Holy Land,* above all, to put an end once and for all
to the senseless spiral of blind violence, and in *the Middle East,*
to extinguish the ominous smoldering of a conflict
which, with the joint efforts of all, can be avoided;
in *Africa,* too, where devastating famines and tragic internal conflicts
are aggravating the already precarious conditions of entire peoples,
although here and there signs of hope are present;
in *Latin America,* in *Asia,* in other parts of the world,
where political, economic, and social crises
disturb the serenity of many families and nations.
May humanity accept the Christmas message of peace!

Adorable mystery of the Incarnate Word!
Together with you, O Virgin Mother, may we stop and reflect
at the manger where the Child lies,
to share your own amazement
at the immense "condescension" of God.
Grant us your own eyes, O Mary,
that we may understand the mystery
hidden within the frail limbs of your Son.

Teach us to recognize his face
in the children of every race and culture.
Help us to be credible witnesses
of his message of peace and love,
so that the men and women of our own time,
still torn by conflicts and unspeakable violence,
may also recognize in the Child
cradled in your arms
the one Savior of the world,
the endless source of that true peace
for which every heart profoundly yearns.

From Address to the Priests of the Diocese of Rome

Dear Brothers in the priesthood, let us never tire of being witnesses and heralds of Christ, let us never be discouraged by the difficulties and obstacles we find either within us, in our human frailty, or in the indifference or lack of understanding of those to whom we are sent, including sometimes the persons who are close to us.

Whenever difficulties and temptations weigh on our hearts, let us very much remember *the greatness of the gift we have received to be able in our turn to "give with joy"* (cf. 2 Cor. 9:7). Indeed, in the confessional above all, but also in our whole ministry, we are *witnesses and instruments of divine mercy*, we are and should be men who know how to *instill hope* and perform a work of *peace and reconciliation*.

Dear Brothers, it is to this that God has called us with a special love of choice, and God deserves our entire confidence: His will for salvation is greater and more powerful than all the sin of the world.

Thank you for this chance to be together. Thank you, too, for *the gift of the book,* fresh from the press, which brings together all the texts of my talks to you at the beginning of Lent, since March 2, 1979. I also hope that this initiative will serve to keep alive and fruitful the dialogue that has been taking place among us in the course of these years.

And it is already twenty-five years! This is the twenty-fifth year. My priestly life began in 1946, with the ordination that I received from the hands of my great predecessor in Kraków, Cardinal Adam Stefan Sapieha.

After twelve years I was called to the episcopate, in 1958. Since 1958, I have spent 45 years of episcopate: that is enough! . . . Of these forty-five years, I spent twenty in Kraków, first as Auxiliary, then as Vicar Capitular, then as Metropolitan Archbishop and

Cardinal; but twenty-five years in Rome! With these figures you see that I have become more Roman than "Krakovian." But all this is Providence.

Today's meeting reminds me of all my meetings with the priests in my first Diocese of Kraków. I must say that there were many more meetings. Above all I was able to visit many parishes. But even in Rome I have visited 300 out of 340. . . . A few are still left! I can say that I am living with this capital that I accumulated more or less in Kraków; a capital of experiences, but not only, also of reflections, of all that my priestly and then episcopal ministry has given me.

I must confess to you parish priests that I have never been a parish priest. I have only been a parochial vicar! And then above all I was a professor in the seminary and university. My experience is more than that of a university chair. But even without a direct, first-hand experience as parish priest, I have always been in touch with many parish priests, and I can say that they have given me the experience that they had. Thus I have made before you, during my twenty-fifth year, a sort of examination of conscience of my priestly life. I am deeply grateful to you for the words you have spoken to me, for the affection you have shown me and, especially, for your prayers, which I always very much need! Thus we have begun our Roman Lent, my twenty-fifth Roman Lent. I wish you a blessed Lent and a happy Easter! Easter is the center not just of our Christian life but also of our priestly life! I offer you my very best wishes.

I warmly bless you all and, with you, I bless the communities entrusted to your care.

MARCH 6, 2003

INDEX OF TITLES
OR FIRST LINES

Abbreviations:
WI = *Words of Inspiration*
IP = *An Invitation to Prayer*
RH = *The Rosary Hour*
LH = *The Loving Heart*

Special thanks to Stanley Browne, Martin Schmukler, Esq., and Marvin Kaplan of Marstan Associates, Ltd. Thanks also to the Libreria Editrice Rogate (LER), Father Nunzio Spinelli, and the Very Reverend Father Leonardo Sapienza, respectively, for the publication and the compilation of the anthologies. And to Rick Garson, Enzo Zullo, Alan R. Kershaw, Advocate of the Apostolic Tribunal of the Roman Rota, Paul Schindler, Esq., Larry Shire, Esq., and Gil Karson, Esq., of Grubman, Indursky and Schindler.

KAROL WOJTYLA, POPE JOHN PAUL II, was born in Wadowice in Poland, in 1920. He studied literature and drama in Kraków and later worked at a stone quarry and at a chemical plant. During the German occupation of Poland in World War II, he began preparing for the priesthood and was ordained in 1946. Wojtyla became bishop of Kraków in 1958, archbishop in 1964, and cardinal in 1967. He was elected Pope in 1978 and was the 264th bishop of Rome.